A Guide to the
Industrial Archaeology
of Europe

A Guide to the Industrial Archaeology of Europe

Kenneth Hudson

Adams & Dart

© 1971, Kenneth Hudson
First published in 1971 by
Adams & Dart, 40 Gay Street, Bath
SBN 239 00035 8
Printed in Great Britain by
R & R Clark Ltd, Edinburgh

Contents

List of Illustrations

Acknowledgements

It is hardly possible to carry out research in twenty-three different countries without the help of many people and I should like to take the opportunity of saying how very grateful I am to them for their kindness.

My special thanks are due to Dr. Georges van den Abeelen (Belgium), Christian Ahlström (Finland), Miss M. A. Asselberghs (Netherlands), Dr. Ulrich Bauche (West Germany), Bernhard and Hilla Becher (West Germany), Dr. Hartwig Beseler (West Germany), Dr. John Butt (Scotland), Dr. Elio Cardoso (Portugal), Dr. H. S. Corran (Republic of Ireland), Neil Cossons (England), M. Daumas (France), Denkmalschutzamt Hamburg, Dr. Michael Ekés (Hungary), Marquis de Espinardo (Spain), Mr. A. Castro Freire (Spain), Anna Grönvik (Finland), Dipl. Ing. L. Heuwing (West Germany), Hungarian Central Technical Library and Documentation Centre, Budapest, Jernbanemuseet, Copenhagen, Jernbanemuseet, Hamar, Anders Jespersen (Denmark), Mgr. E. Krygier (Poland), Landbrugsmuseet, Copenhagen, Mrs. S. Levai (Hungary), K. Mawhinney (Republic of Ireland), Dr. W. A. McCutcheon (Northern Ireland), Mr. A. Moser (Switzerland), Museo del Ferrocarril (Spain), Prof. Dr. Ing. Hans Nadler (D.D.R.), Dipl. Ing. R. Niederhuemer (Austria), Marie Nisser (Sweden), John Papaioannou (Greece), Professor Hugo Pipping (Finland), Michael Rix (England), Bruno Rüttiman (Switzerland), Carlo Sauro (Italy), Gunnar Sillen (Sweden), Dr. Vasilye Simia (Yugoslavia), Dr. Norman Smith (England), Sigvard Strandh (Sweden), Verein Deutschen Ingenieure (West Germany), Dr. Jiri Vondra (Czechoslovakia), Dr. Otfried Wagenbreth (D.D.R.).

I owe two particular debts of gratitude, one to the Leverhulme Trust, who made me a grant which greatly eased the burden of travelling expenses, and the other to Miss Ann Nicholls, who carried out an extensive

x

and often frustrating correspondence for me and sorted out and typed a manuscript of more than ordinary difficulty, containing strange words from most of the languages of Europe.

The following photographs are the copyright of:

Ålands Museum 29–31; James Austin 17,18; Bernhard and Hilla Becher 51, 54, 58–61; Courtauld Institute of Art 36–38, 63; Deutsche Fotothek, Dresden 3; French Government Tourist Office 2; Greek National Tourist Office 4; Landesamt für Denkmal-Pflege, Schleswig-Holstein 28; Eric de Marré 6, 7, 14–16; Dr. W. A. McCutcheon 20, 32; William Morris 9; Netherlands National Tourist Office 27; Marie Nisser 11, 41, 43; Novosti Press Agency 71, 72; Photo Ch. Leva, Brussels 50; Photohaus Zümbuhl, St Gallen 57; Polish Travel Office 34; Portuguese State Office 10; Franz Schneider 5; South West Picture Agency Ltd. 19; Spanish National Tourist Office 1; Staatliche Landesbildstelle, Hamburg 12; Prins Eugene Waldemarsudde 33; Michael Wagen 8; Josiah Wedgwood & Sons, Ltd. 62; West Midlands Photo Services, Ltd. 42

Introduction

In Britain the terms 'industrial archaeology' and 'industrial monuments' are generally understood and accepted. Other countries tend to fight a little shy of 'industrial archaeology' and prefer to speak of 'technological monuments'. In either case what is meant is the material relating to yesterday's manufacturing and transport which has survived, more or less intact, on its original site. Most of these structures or pieces of machinery date from the eighteenth and nineteenth centuries, although some are earlier and some, especially in the case of the newer industries like electronics, aircraft and plastics, are considerably later.

National policy towards the preservation of such monuments varies a great deal. In some countries – Italy and Spain are good examples – industrial monuments have a relatively low prestige, by comparison with the classical and artistic antiquities which are considered to be the nation's great glory and, apart from the sunshine, the major tourist attraction. In others – the German Democratic Republic and Czechoslovakia, for instance – industrial monuments are very highly valued, as evidence and symbols of the history of the working class, and receive appropriate financial support, while castles, churches and the noble houses of the rich are correspondingly played down.

Most European countries are in a position somewhere between that of Italy and East Germany. They have a tradition of devoting public money to restoring and preserving certain kinds of religious, political and social monuments and, within the past ten years, they have become aware, or been made aware, that attitudes to history have been changing and that efforts to record and preserve notable railway stations, stationary steam engines, canals and woollen mills, to take only four examples, should be made before this material disappears for ever. With public funds as limited as they are everywhere, what has happened in most cases is that governments have given industrial monuments their blessing and included them in their lists of historical items to be preserved, but have provided little or no money in order to allow this preservation to become a reality.

In Belgium, Germany, Holland, France, Britain and other Western European countries where industrialisation took place on a considerable scale during the eighteenth and nineteenth centuries and where industrial monuments are, compared with, say, Portugal or Greece, thick on the ground, very little money indeed has been provided from public funds in order to protect even the finest and most important of these monuments from decay or disappearance. To some extent, this reflects uncertainty as to whether such monuments are likely to be of sufficient interest to the public as tourist attractions to justify spending money on them. There is the further complication that industrial monuments tend to be large, and are therefore very expensive to repair and maintain. One cannot usually recoup any of this expenditure by finding a new use for the building. A bridge or gasworks cannot very well be turned to other purposes, whereas a country mansion can be used as a school or an industrial research head-quarters, a castle can be converted into flats, and services are still held in restored churches and cathedrals. In general neither governments nor tourist organisations are very clear about what kind of attention industrial monuments demand of them.

This does not mean that preservation is an impossibility. If an industrial building is architecturally remarkable, if it is not in the way of any urgently needed rebuilding or replanning, and if it has captured the interest of some body of enthusiasts willing to campaign on its behalf, survival is possible. In England, for example, the Victorian Society is a powerful pressure group, with friends in high places, and may well have prevented the demolition or remodelling of St Pancras Station in London, just as organised pleasure-boaters may prevent Bristol Corporation from filling in the abandoned City Docks.

There are fashions in beauty, and although old industrial buildings no longer carry quite the stigma they did even twenty years ago, they are un-likely to be regarded with quite the same romantic affection as a castle or a cathedral, at least by the general public. Many factory chimneys are objects of great beauty, but, as pointers to Heaven, they are not usually given the same prestige and survival value as church spires. An interest in most kinds of industrial monument reflects a well-balanced mind and an educated taste. Such an interest, at least in North-West Europe, is a good deal more widespread today than it was even a decade ago, but it needs to be nourished by an equal willingness on the part of governments to provide money, authority and expertise to prevent historically significant industrial material from falling victim to the demolition and the scrap metal merchant.

Fortunately, governments are not the only source of funds for preserving industrial monuments. Much has already been accomplished by individual firms sufficiently enlightened and public-spirited to want to keep their history and traditions alive, by preservation societies and by local authorities. What has been done in this way has achieved something, but not enough, to produce a change of attitude in Ministries. Industrial monuments are much more respectable now than they were ten or twenty years ago.

In every country, there are differences of opinion about the wisdom of trying to preserve the larger and less moveable industrial monuments. Photographs, plans and models shown in a museum in conjunction with, wherever possible, such pieces of the original plant as can be transferred are thought, by some well-informed people, to be the limit of possibility and reasonableness. Anything which does not fit in with this approach is inevitably doomed, and rightly so. It is obviously true that we cannot possibly hope to preserve more than a tiny fraction of superannuated machines and industrial buildings. If we tried to keep everything of interest, the country would rapidly become clogged up. The memorials of dead workers would crowd out the activities of living workers. There are, even so, two strong objections to the museum-or-nothing theory. One can be stated in the form of a question. Would looking at a model of St Paul's Cathedral be the equivalent of standing inside St Paul's Cathedral? The other objection is concerned with historical balance. If we preserve only non-industrial buildings for posterity, we cannot put the technological achievements of our ancestors into their proper perspective. Only by actually seeing them where they were built can we appreciate the scale and workmanship of these old bridges and factories. Left to itself, our imagination plays tricks with us.

This is not to say, of course, that museums are undesirable institutions. They are an indispensable means of remembering and interpreting the past, and most of the objects we manage to save from destruction will necessarily have to be brought together into the safety and expert care of collections. Many museums, in any case, are delightful places and one would want as many people as possible to enjoy the pleasure of visiting them. All that is being suggested, however, is that industrial museums and industrial monuments can enjoy a peaceful and fruitful co-existence, in just the same way as archaeological monuments and archaeological museums have done for a very long time. Only the most eccentric person would suggest blowing up the Parthenon, levelling out a round barrow or driving a road through the middle of a Roman villa site, simply because these are inconvenient objects to remove to a museum. The principle is accepted that some archaeological remains demand museum treatment and that others are properly safeguarded where they have always been. In this respect, the remains of industrial archaeology are no different from those of any other branch of archaeology.

A Guide to the Industrial Archaeology of Europe

In writing the present book, it has been assumed that a revolution in taste has occurred and that industrial-technological monuments can give a good deal of pleasure to a good many people. It has also been taken for granted that the same person can be equally interested in looking round an eighteenth-century salt mine, a Victorian waterworks, and a medieval church or castle. What we are saying, in effect, is this: the country or the district you are visiting contains a good many more interesting things than the guidebooks and the tourist agencies might lead you to believe. The more you extend your range of places to see, the more interesting your tour is likely to be.

This has not been an easy book to write, partly because it has no predecessor – the internationally-minded industrial archaeologist is almost terrifyingly on his own – partly because the area to be covered is so enormous and partly because of the great dangers and absurdities involved in setting one country by the side of another. The industrialisation of Europe has been an extremely uneven business, dependent on raw materials, size of population, climate and political pressures. The more one knows about a country's history and development, the more significant every factory and railway and shipyard becomes, no matter what its age. The astonishing industrial growth of Yugoslavia and Hungary since 1945 is just as fascinating as the decaying Lancashire cotton industry during the same period. Both have their monuments, but the monuments in Yugoslavia and Hungary are more recent than those of Lancashire in its cotton days. And just as one cannot make proper sense of a new steelworks in Eastern Hungary without seeing the tiny watermills which represented the economy of the area only a few years earlier, so one has to put the old Cunard headquarters in Liverpool by the side of the new Ford factory a few miles away, the abandoned railway by the side of the new motorway.

This guide is best used by allowing the past and the present to flow into one another wherever one happens to be. I have tried to do no more than indicate the kind of material the visitor should be looking for and to locate, in each country, a small number of the more interesting monuments of industry and transport, so that the stranger can get his bearings without too much frustration and waste of time. There can be few tourists who feel no interest in the local inhabitants, and it is natural enough to wonder how the people one sees earn a living. Industrial monuments help to answer this question. They belong to social history as much as to the history of technology and it does no harm to visit the watermills, the forges, the mines and the tunnels with the workers, rather than the machines, uppermost in one's thoughts.

Author's Note

In the list provided at the end of each section the more important sites are located in three ways:

(1) By giving the geographical co-ordinates, e.g. 59.55N 30.25E.
(2) By using the grid given in the appropriate handbook issued by the Automobile Association, e.g. Map 15 EF 34. This gives motorists the grid square in which the site is to be found.
(3) In the case of villages and isolated sites not indicated in the AA handbooks, by giving the nearest town of any size.

The museums referred to at the beginning of each section are those which have substantial collections illustrating the history of industry and technology. The full address is given wherever there might otherwise be some difficulty in finding the museum in question.

There are few local or regional museums without material to show how industry and transport have developed in the area, and many cover this particular aspect very well. The present guide assumes that visitors will see what local museums have to offer in the way of general background and orientation, and draws attention only to the more specialised collections.

It should, however, be borne in mind that a museum is not always a museum in the English sense. In Eastern Europe especially, what is described as a museum may turn out to be an exhibition of entirely modern products. On the other hand, what appears in the list as an open-air museum can usually be relied upon to include houses, churches, mills and workshops which have been transferred from their original site to the museum grounds. There is no open-air museum known to the author which does not provide useful and interesting documentation of the technology and economic activity of past generations, although some museums are naturally more rewarding to visit than others.

Much the same is true of naval and maritime museums. In some the emphasis is heavily on models, drawings and pictures of ships, but in others there is a great deal of information about ports, harbours and dockside facilities. The industrial and transport archaeologist will be much better pleased with some maritime museums than with others.

In a pioneering guide of this kind, where research has covered 23 countries and has been spread over a number of years, there will inevitably be some sites, monuments and museums which have not been brought to the author's attention, and others which no longer have the same features. The author and publishers would be grateful for information which would provide additional or more up-to-date material for subsequent editions.

AUSTRIA

Austria is well provided with technological monuments, despite the war-time destruction between 1939 and 1945, mainly in the Eastern part of the country. During the period of the Austro-Hungarian Empire industrial development was largely confined to the cities of Vienna, Graz and Linz, although the timber and mineral resources of the eastern provinces were considerably exploited. The scale of Austrian industry has changed greatly since 1945, in an attempt to overcome the difficulties which have plagued the country ever since the Treaty of Versailles dismembered the old Empire and made economic nonsense of Central Europe. As part of this general process of growth and modernisation, many of the older and smaller industrial enterprises have been shut down or absorbed into larger units.

MUSEUMS

The National Technical Museum (Technisches Museum für Industrie und Gewerbe, Mariahilferstrasse 212), in *Vienna*, was established at the beginning of the present century; however, it has been starved of funds for many years and the collections are, as a result, not adequately housed or displayed – at least not by today's standards. It also provides a home for a Railway Museum and a Postal and Telegraphic Museum. There is also a much bigger and better Railway Museum at Linz.

There are several open-air museums in Austria. The Freilichtmuseum at *Mondsee* contains a watermill, a steeping-tank for flax, a pottery kiln and a 'smokehouse'. A new museum at *Gross-Stübing*, in Styria, has farm steads and rural workshops, while the Glasmuseum at *Gmünd* (Stadtplatz

34) shows the history of glassmaking in Lower Austria since the fourteenth century. There are two museums with good collections for the history of wine-production in Lower Austria, one at *Krems-an-der-Donau* (Theaterplatz 9) and the other at *Retz*, and there is a weaving museum (Webermuseum, Kirchenplatz) at *Haslach-an-der-Mühl*.

IRON INDUSTRY

Austria has had an important iron industry for several centuries. The most important source of ore is the *Erzberg* (Iron Mountain), in Styria. During the Middle Ages iron-ore was taken from surface workings and quarries. Then at the beginning of the nineteenth century a carefully-designed system of mines and tunnels was developed. In the 1870s, however, a change was made to surface mining up the side of the mountain, where thirty terraces, each about eighty feet high, form a giant staircase. As the ore is removed, the summit of the Erzberg is gradually being reduced in height. Most of the ore is sent untreated to the blast-furnaces at Donauwitz and Linz.

There are many memorials of the earlier days of the iron industry. At *Eisenerz*, an old mining town in the Salzkammergut, a bell in the Schichtturm ('Shift-tower') used to be rung to tell the miners when the next shift was due to start. At *Lienz* in the East Tyrol there is a seventeenth-century forge, with much of its original equipment, and at *Oberzeiring* in Styria, an old iron-mine (Schaubergwerk) can be visited. In Lower Austria and Styria, around the *Ötscher Mountains*, there were once many small foundries and forges, using iron-ore from the great Erzberg mountain range of which the Ötscher forms part, but none of them has been preserved.

Salla in Styria was formerly a great centre of the scythe-making industry. Styrian scythe-blades had a world-wide reputation, and the ruins of a number of the little factories which made the scythe blades can be seen along the river which runs through a ravine here. The Heimathaus Steyr Museum (Am Grünmarkt 26) at *Steyr*, in Upper Austria, has a fully-equipped scythe-smithy.

The industrial town of *Bruck-an-der-Mur*, in Styria, was a centre for wealthy iron-masters and traders in metal. An elegant memorial of the earlier iron industry is to be seen here – a wrought-iron well, made in 1626 by a local workman, Hans Prasser. It is claimed, with good reason, to be the greatest Styrian achievement in iron-work.

COPPER, SILVER AND GOLD MINING

Mühlbach, in the Salzach valley, was producing copper in the Bronze Age, and although operations have now ceased there, evidence is still to be seen of the nineteenth-century processing plant at the Muterberg works, near *Bischofshofen*. The present glass and engineering industries were established after copper mining and smelting came to an end.

Silver and gold mining was established early in Austria, although little is carried on today. In Carinthia, at *Döllach-im-Mölltal*, there is a museum which gives the history of gold mining in the Tauern mountains, and at the church at *Bad Hofgastein* numbers of tombstones of exceptionally fine workmanship bear the effigies of the rich owners of the gold and silver mines, recalling the industry's prosperous period in the sixteenth and seventeenth centuries, when the local mining of precious metals brought large contributions to church funds. At *Oberzeiring*, in Upper Austria, the disused silver mine can be visited, on payment of a fee.

SALT MINING

The Austrian salt-mines are famous. Those of the *Dürrnberg* have been worked since Neolithic times, and are still in production, but only as a tourist attraction (from 1 May to 30 September). *Hallein*, near Salzburg, was developed from the thirteenth century onwards, around the salt pans laid out on an island in the Salzach to evaporate brine from the Dürrnberg mines. The Stadtmuseum at Hallein contains a number of models of the salt and iron-ore mines and at *Solbad Hall*, in the Tyrol, the Mining Museum (Bergmuseum) has an underground display showing the techniques of salt-mining. At *Perneck*, 4.8 kilometres from Bad Ischl, the salt-works are open to visitors, and at *Hallstatt* in Upper Austria the salt-galleries can also be visited from 1 May to 30 September. The very extensive and dry salt mines near *Altausee* were used to store art-collections during the Second World War, and at *Badgastein* a curative establishment, where the treatment includes taking the waters, has been set up in abandoned mine galleries opening above the Böckstein.

POTTERY

The pottery industry has been much rationalised since 1945. A good example of this is the ÖSPAG pottery works at *Wilhelmsburg* in Lower Austria. This was established in 1796 as a development of an older hand-work business, by an Englishman, Martin Leinwatter, who had had experience at Wedgwood's. The factory is now large and fully modernised, producing both sanitary ware and porcelain. Parts of the older buildings are still to be seen, but the plant as a whole bears no resemblance to the nineteenth-century pottery.

TRANSPORT AND CIVIL ENGINEERING

Transport in Austria has had to face considerable difficulties, mainly because of the mountainous nature of much of the country. The railways were expensive to build, with much bridging and tunnelling, as anyone travelling by train from Switzerland to Salzburg is likely to realise, and – apart from the Danube – there was little help to be obtained from waterways. On the other hand, the large number of mountainous streams and fast-running rivers have provided a useful supply of power, both for electricity and in the old days for waterwheels. Austria is full of notable achievements in civil engineering, and in roadbuilding one could instance the road leading to the *Semmering Pass*, which was ingeniously relaid in 1842 on the Gloggnitz slope, to give a maximum gradient of 1 in 7.

WATERMILLS

The Danube has already been mentioned in connection with transport, and in *Vienna* it was also a source of power, notably for the boat-mills (Schiffsmühlen). These floating mills, one containing the waterwheel and machinery and the other used for storage, existed in Vienna in the seventeenth century on what was then the main river, but which was later bypassed and known as the Old Danube (Alte Donau). The mills were known as the Emperor's Mills (Kaisermühlen), and the name lives on as a street-name in Stadlau, in the 22nd District. When the mills were shifted to the new cut, between 1869 and 1875, there were 23 on the right bank of the river, above the Nordwestbahn railway bridge, and 33 along the Kriauer and Freudenauer embankments on the left bank. The group on the right bank had all disappeared by 1858, but the last of those on the left bank survived until 1935.

Most of the Vienna mills, however, were fixed, not floating. There were six mill-streams running off the river Wien, a tributary of the Danube, and although the buildings of the last of these mills, the Glutmühle in the Utendorfergasse, 11th–14th District, were still standing in 1967 they have since been demolished. The bed of the mill-stream can, however, be seen in places near the track of the Westbahn.

Location of sites - **Austria***

Altausee	47.38N 13.46E	Map 15 CD 23
Badgastein	47.07N 13.09E	Map 15 BC 12
Bad Hofgastein	47.10N 13.06E	Map 15 BC 12

Bischofshofen	47.25N 13.13E	Map 15 BC 23
Bruck-an-der-Mur	47.25N 15.16E	Map 15 EF 23
Eisenerz, south-east of Hieflau	47.33N 14.53E	Map 15 DE 23
Erzberg, north of Mariazell	47.47N 15.20E	Map 15 EF 34
Hallein	47.41N 13.06E	Map 15 BC 23
Hallstatt	47.34N 13.39E	Map 15 CD 23
Lienz	46.50N 12.47E	Map 14 BC 12
Mühlbach, west-south-west of Bischofshofen	47.22N 13.08E	Map 15 BC 23
Oberzeiring, north of St Georgen	47.12N 14.30E	Map 15 DE 23
Ötscher Mountains	47.52N 15.13E	Map 15 DE 34
Perneck, near Bad Ischl	47.43N 13.37E	Map 15 CD 23
Salla, north-west of Köflach	47.06N 14.58E	Map 15 DE 12
Semmering Pass	47.38N 15.49E	Map 15 EF 23
Steyr	48.04N 14.25E	Map 15 DE 34
Vienna	48.13N 16.20E	Map 15 FG 34
Wilhelmsburg	48.07N 15.37E	Map 15 EF 34

* *A.A. Continental Handbook, 1970–1*

BELGIUM

The industrialisation of Belgium began relatively early. There were a number of reasons for this: large deposits of coal, easy access to the Ruhr and to the industrial areas of Northern France, a long tradition of handicrafts and technical skill, close connections with Britain, adequate capital. Belgium has drawn heavily and profitably on the expertise and business acumen of her neighbours. One is constantly reminded of this by the number of foreign – and especially English – names which occur in the names of companies, and sometimes in an even more concrete way. In *Liège*, for example, there is a square called the Place Cockerill, and a plaque here reads: 'John Cockerill donna un grand essor à l'industrie sidérurgique liégoise' (John Cockerill gave the Liège steel industry new momentum). Cockerill was the son of an English merchant who migrated to Belgium in the late eighteenth century. He established workshops at Seraing, near Liège, in 1817 and built his first coke-fired furnace there in 1823. When he died in 1840 his industrial empire was reorganised as a public company, with the government holding 50 per cent. of the shares. The great Seraing works is still in use, modernised and much enlarged.

MUSEUMS

It is remarkable that such a heavily-industrialised country such as Belgium should have no national museum of industry and technology. This probably reflects a deeply-ingrained dislike of any form of national institution. Unlike the Dutch, the Belgians have little respect for a central government, a fact which reveals itself in many interesting ways, including a widespread disregard for the law even amongst the most highly respectable people. There are, however, a number of well-planned and well-arranged local museums containing industrial material, such as the Maison Tournaisienne in *Tournai* and the Musée Gaumais at *Virton*. One of the most curious of these local museums is the Brewer's House (Maison des Brasseurs, Brouwersstraat 20) in *Antwerp*. In the mid-sixteenth century small dead-end canals (vlieten) were dug, running at right-angles to the Scheldt. One of these was the Brewers' Canal (Brouwersvliet). Beer was made from the canal water, which was taken from the canal to a central reservoir in the Brewers' House and piped from there to twenty-four separate breweries. A horse-driven bucket mill was used to raise the water to the reservoir, and besides the reservoir and pumping equipment the house contains stables and a meeting room for the brewers.

Also in *Antwerp* is the splendidly-preserved headquarters of the great seventeenth-century printer, Christopher Plantin. These buildings, now the Musée Plantin-Moretus at Vrijdagmarkt 22, contain the offices, shop, press-room, type-foundry, composing-room and proof-readers' room, all in their original condition. At 19 Suikerrui in *Antwerp* there is a Cooperage Museum in the wine cellar, which dates from the twelfth century, where one can see a collection of old coopers' tools, while at Koningin Astrid Plein 26, not far from the main railway station, there are showrooms and workshops relating to the diamond industry. The Museum of Folklore in *Gent*, at Kraanlei 41, includes craftsmen's workshops.

There is an open-air museum at *Bokrijk*, near Genk, with an emphasis on agricultural buildings, but with a number of examples of mills also. These include an eighteenth-century octagonal wooden mill, with a moveable head, from Schulen in Limburg; a very large pivoting windmill (1788) from Mol-Millegem; and a watermill from Lummen-Rekhoven in Kempen. This last mill is a composite exhibit – the building comes from Lummen and the mechanism from the Rooiermolen in Gruitrode. The museum also includes an oil-mill (1702) from Ellikom, Kempen, and a rope-making workshop from Oevelberg, St Peters-Lille. At *Doel* an early seventeenth-century windmill (1614) has been converted into a small museum. *Nivelles* has a Mill Museum, including examples of both watermills and windmills, and an early forge, probably from the late eighteenth century, is preserved on the same site. At *Ellezelles*, in Hainaut, a famous post-mill, the Chat Sauvage (1750), has been preserved in working order by the tourist federation of the province, the present owners.

TRANSPORT Road and Rail

British engineers and financiers played a great part in building up Belgium's industries during the eighteenth and nineteenth centuries, and the connections with French and German entrepreneurs were equally close. This is well shown by the Grand Luxembourg Railway, inaugurated in 1858, which for a number of years had a British majority on its board of directors. The railway, as far as the British were concerned, if not the Belgians, was part of a grand design to build a railway from Ostend to the Far East by the shortest possible route. It was to be the route for the Indian Mail (La Malle des Indes), and one of the original stations on this line, at Arlon, was transferred to *Mellier*, where it can still be seen.

In *Brussels* there is a railway museum at the Gare du Nord, and a large section of the Musées Royaux d'Art et d'Histoire in the Parc Cinquantenaire is devoted to horse-drawn vehicles, cars and bicycles. There is also a tramway museum at *Schepdael*, seven miles from Brussels.

Among other notable transport monuments that should certainly be mentioned is the magnificent Central Station in *Antwerp*. Designed in the grand tradition by Delacenserie and completed in 1905, its dome rises to a height of 65.4 metres.

TRANSPORT Canals

The Charleroi Canal was originally built between 1827 and 1832 to carry ships of only 300 tons, but since its reconstruction, completed in 1960, it now takes ships of 1,350 tons from Charleroi to Brussels. It has a rise of 1,148 metres, with 37 locks, and interesting technical features can be seen at *Ronquières*, including an inclined plane 1389 metres long which raises barges 66.6 metres in tanks of water measuring 91.4 by 11.8 metres. Modernisation on this scale is typical of the great importance Belgium has given to its canals, but there have been political complications. The Zuid-Willens or Maastricht s'Hertogenbosch Canal, for instance, was completed in 1826, during the time of the United Netherlands, and more than half of it is now in Holland. In 1844 the newly independent Belgium built from this canal, at Bocholt, a new canal running entirely through Belgian territory, the Meuse-Schelat or Kempen Canal. The Albert Canal, between Kanne and Eben-Emaal, incorporated a section of the Kempen Canal; completed in 1852, it was reconstructed in the 1930s to take ships of 2,000 tons. It is 129 kilometres long, and six has sets of triple locks and a single set at *Monsin*, near Liège: there is now a continuous ship-canal link between Liège and Antwerp.

Another important Belgian canal, the Brussels-Rupel, also known as the Willebroek, was originally built in the sixteenth century, but has been enlarged and transformed since, and allows vessels to reach the centre of Brussels from the Scheldt. Also deepened and widened since its construction in 1827 is the Gent-Terneuzen ship canal. Hydraulic lifts can be seen on the Central Canal at *Houdeng*, in Hainaut.

TRANSPORT   Docks

Antwerp Docks have been constructed at various periods and now cover a very large area, more than 1,300 hectares. Several of the nineteenth-century docks are still in use, the earliest being the Bonaparte Dock (1811) and the Willem Dock (1813). The Mole at *Zeebrugge* was completed in 1884, and runs out to sea in the shape of a crescent moon for 2.4 kilometres, protecting the entrance to the ship canal. Zeebrugge is linked to Bruges by a 12-kilometre canal built between 1856 and 1907.

IRON INDUSTRY

The Musée de la Vie Wallonne, in the Cours des Mineurs at *Liège*, has a water-driven hammer (*maka*) from the last forge in the province of Liège to operate with such a hammer. This was at *Chaudfontaine* and the forge building can still be easily identified in the main street of the village, backing on to the river Vesdre. The sluices and the flume for feeding water to the wheel have survived. Another monument to the old iron industry is the Fourneau Saint-Michel, 6.4 kilometres from *St Hubert*. A museum has been arranged around the eighteenth-century foundry (1771), which was restored in 1968, and a somewhat incongruous workshop for making wooden shoes also forms part of the museum. The ironworks was founded by Dom Nicolas Spirlet, a Benedictine monk.

An excellent museum of the Belgian iron industry in its charcoal days was developed at Vennes, near Liège, between 1951 and 1955, by a very old-established company making water-pipes, the Compagnie Générale des Conduites d'Eau. The museum was established in an old mill-building and the collection was limited to material from before 1830, the date when coke was first used in a blast furnace in Belgium. It includes a blast-furnace, a wooden air-compressor for the blast, and a maka, in addition to many smaller pieces of equipment and objects made of iron. In 1967, with a change of management, the collection was moved to another building in the neighbourhood, at *Longdoz*, and is now in the care of the Société Métallurgique d'Espérance-Longdoz. The new title of the museum is the Centre Cultural du Fer et du Charbon.

COAL INDUSTRY

The coal-mining area of the *Borinage*, close to the French border is, in a sense, its own monument. Production has greatly declined during the past 25 years and the number of men employed is only a fraction of what it was, yet for something like a century and a half the industrial prosperity of Belgium was founded on coal mined in the Borinage, and one drives through its half-abandoned landscape now with an inescapable feeling of the harsh, tough past.

The most remarkable industrial monument in this coal-mining area, if not in all Europe, is undoubtedly *Le Grand-Hornu*, an industrial village built by the coal owner Henri De Gorge-Legrand, between 1819 and 1840 (see plate 50). The centre-piece of the village is a very large oval forum, which is colonnaded and has a statue of the founder in the middle. Behind the colonnade are workshops and stores, while streets of houses for the work-people complete the scheme, which was the work of the well-known architect, Bruno Renard. Work ceased at Le Grand-Hornu in the 1950s and the buildings have become considerably dilapidated since then; however, a recent proposal has been made to establish a Belgian National Museum of Industry and Technology here and it is difficult to imagine a more suitable or more impressive site.

GLASS-MAKING

Glass-manufacture has been important in Belgium for 300 years, centred from the beginning in the province of Hainaut, and more particularly in the area of *Charleroi*. During the eighteenth century Hainaut made mainly bottles and common window-glass. In the nineteenth century the manufacture of window-glass became concentrated into increasingly large units; it was mechanised during the ten years before the outbreak of the First World War. In 1914 the Fourcault factory at Dampremy became the first in the world to use continuous casting machines. There are now only two companies involved in the window-glass side of the industry, both of which are very large, and one making bottles. Modernisation and rebuilding have removed nearly all the monuments of the old, small-scale industry, but one that has survived is the glass-works at *Barbençon*. These modest buildings are of brick, with slate roofs, and date from the first half of the seventeenth century. There is a Glass Museum in *Liège*, at 13 quai de Maastricht.

POTTERY

The Boch family, who were originally iron-founders in Lorraine, established a pottery at Septfontaines in Luxembourg in 1767. However, the division of Belgium and Luxembourg in 1839 created marketing problems, and in 1851 a factory was opened at *La Louvière* in Hainaut, where there was coal, and good transport by means of a branch of the Charleroi

Canal. The business became very large and the premises have been extended many times, but the original building can still be seen in the middle of the present complex.

DAMS

There are two famous twentieth-century dams that should be mentioned, one at *Gileppe* and the other at *Eupen*. The Gileppe dam, with its 196-acre lake and surrounding wooded hills, is 228 metres long and is surmounted by a 12.2-metre statue of a lion. The Eupen dam is much larger, 63 metres in height, and holds back an artificial lake of 26,000 acres.

QUARRYING

At *Soignies*, between Brussels and Mons, are the famous bluestone (*pierre bleue*) quarries, which have been worked since the twelfth century and are nowadays in production on a very large scale. This uncommon type of limestone has a number of very excellent qualities which endear it to the builder; it stands up well to frost, damp and smoke, works easily, has an exceptionally high compression-strength, and can be sold at a very competitive price. Its blue-grey surface becomes white at the points where it is struck by a hammer or chisel, and a wide range of effects can be obtained by different methods of dressing the stone. It has been extensively used in the Brussels-Tournai-Mons area for several centuries and can be seen in a great variety of old buildings, often combined with brick.

Location of sites - **Belgium***

Antwerp	51.13N	4.25E	Map 10 EF 23
Barbençon, south-east of Beaumont	50.13N	4.17E	Map 10 EF 12
Bokrijk, near Genk	50.58N	5.30E	Map 10 FG 23
Charleroi	50.25N	4.27E	Map 10 EF 12
Chaudfontaine	50.35N	5.38E	Map 10 FG 12
Doel, north-east of Antwerp	51.19N	4.16E	Map 10 EF 23
Ellezelles, east-south-east of Ronse	50.44N	3.41E	Map 10 DE 12

Eupen	50.38N	6.02E	Map 10 FG 12
Gent	51.02N	3.42E	Map 10 DE 23
Gileppe, east of Verviers	50.35N	6.00E	Map 10 FG 12
Houdeng, north-east of Mons	50.29N	4.10E	Map 10 EF 12
La Louvière, east of Mons	50.28N	4.11E	Map 10 EF 12
Le Grand-Hornu	50.27N	3.50E	Map 10 DE 12
Liège	50.38N	5.35E	Map 10 FG 12
Mellier, south-east of Neufchâteau	49.43N	5.32E	Map 13 FG 56
Monsin, west of Liège	50.38N	5.35E	Map 10 FG 23
Nivelles	50.36N	4.20E	Map 10 EF 12
Ronquières, Charleroi Canal	50.37N	4.13E	Map 10 EF 12
Schepdaal, west of Brussels	50.50N	4.12E	Map 10 EF 23
Soignies	50.35N	4.04E	Map 10 DE 12
St Hubert	50.01N	5.23E	Map 13 FG 56
Tournai	50.36N	3.24E	Map 10 DE 12
Vennes, east of Liège	50.38N	5.35E	Map 10 FG 23
Virton, south-west of Arlon	49.34N	5.32E	Map 13 FG 56
Zeebrugge	51.20N	3.12E	Map 10 DE 23

* *A.A. Continental Handbook, 1970–1*

1 El Acueducto, Segovia, Spain. Built *c.* AD 80, to bring water to Segovia and restored in the fifteenth century for the same purpose, this aqueduct has been, in a very real sense, the city's life-line since Roman times. (*see page* 132)

2 Pont du Gard, France. 18 BC. This splendidly situated Roman viaduct is in a remarkably good state of preservation. Its giant blocks have defied two thousand years of war, weather and local hunger for building materials, and it is one of the major tourist attractions of Provence. (*see page* 66)

3 Göltzchtalbrücke, German Democratic Republic. 1845–51. One of the most impressive of Europe's railway viaducts, which reproduces, for strictly practical reasons, the design developed and perfected by the Romans nearly 2000 years earlier. (*see page* 77)

4 Corinth Canal, Greece. Begun AD 67, completed 1893. For the Roman engineers, with only slaves and hand tools, it would have been a feat approaching
the construction of the Pyramids; for their successors in the nineteenth century
it was a considerable problem, even with the help of explosives. (*see page* 83)

5 Kapellbrücke, Lucerne, Switzerland. 1333. One of the finest and best-known of
Switzerland's covered bridges. The tower adjoining the bridge was originally a
water-tower and subsequently became the headquarters of one of the city's
trade guilds. (*see page* 152)

6 Ironbridge, near Coalbrookdale, England. 1779. The first iron bridge to be built anywhere in the world. It is now seriously threatened with collapse, as a consequence of the banks forcing the abutments inwards. (*see page* 23)

7 Ironbridge: detail of construction, showing timber-jointing techniques imitated
in iron. What the designers did, in effect,
was to copy a wooden bridge in iron, even
to the extent of having mortised and
pegged joints.

8 Clifton Suspension Bridge, Bristol, England. Begun 1836, completed 1864, using chains from Hungerford Bridge. The design was Brunel's, but, owing to chronic shortage of money, the bridge was not finished until after his death.

9 Victoria Bridge, Bath, England. 1842. This small bridge is very important in the history of civil engineering. Its suspension rods are inclined, not vertical, from the main cable. This system holds the bridge more rigidly than the traditional method and is a satisfactory way of dealing with wind pressure in exposed situations.

10 Dom Luis I Bridge, Oporto, Portugal. 1880. An early steel bridge, by the French engineer, T. Seyrig, who collaborated with Gustave Eiffel to build the Maria Pia bridge at Lisbon. (*see page* 123)

BRITISH ISLES
England, Scotland, Wales

Britain was the first industrial nation, but her role as an industrial pioneer has been frequently exaggerated. The remarkable achievements of British engineers and entrepreneurs during the second half of the eighteenth century and the first half of the nineteenth gave rise to great technical advances in certain key branches of technology – notably iron, textiles, railways, steam-engines and machine tools – but British superiority even in these specialities was becoming much less marked by 1850, and there were many other fields, such as the design of roads and bridges, mining, timber-processing, chemicals and concrete technology where other European countries were in the forefront during much of the nineteenth century. One aspect of the industrial revolution was undeniably pioneered by Britain – huge, hideous, dirty, smoke-polluted conurbations – and it was the size, productivity and inhuman horror of these new industrial areas which, paradoxically, gave Britain its original reputation for being a thoroughgoing, efficient, wideawake industrial nation, a reputation which it has never wholly lost, despite much subsequent evidence to the contrary.

Britain's industrial monuments are very numerous and no apology is needed for the amount of space devoted to them in the present book. They fall into two categories: those which belong to the earlier, largely eighteenth-century, stages of industrialisation and are to be found mainly in rural areas and in smaller towns; and those which are later and were sited in the major industrial complexes such as Manchester and Birmingham, which characterised the manufacturing pattern in the nineteenth century. On the whole, the earlier monuments have survived a good deal better than the later, largely because buildings in big cities are under much greater economic pressure to justify their continued existence.

MUSEUMS

The Science Museum at Kensington in *London* has one of the best tech-nological collections in the world. It was established in the 1850s, as a symbol of Victorian England's immense confidence in its prosperity and industrial destiny, and has expanded steadily ever since, although it now faces serious problems of space and finance and is often compelled to re-ject important material which it would very much like to acquire. The Science Museum now controls the Museum of British Transport, at present at Clapham, in south London, but shortly to be transferred to new premises in York, where there is at present a railway museum. Another railway museum, concerned entirely with the history of the Great Western Railway, is at *Swindon*.

There are excellent industrial and technical collections at the regional and local museums: in *Birmingham* (City Museum, Newhall Street, Birmingham 3), *Bristol* (City Museum, Queen's Road, Bristol 8), *Cardiff* (National Museum of Wales, Cathays Park), *Edinburgh* (Royal Scottish Museum, Chambers Street, Edinburgh 1), *Glasgow* (City Art Gallery and Museum, Kelvingrove, Glasgow C3), *Liverpool* (City Museum, William Brown Street, Liverpool 3), and *Manchester* (Manchester Museum of Science and Technology, 97 Grosvenor Street, Manchester 1). A number of other towns have museums or sections of museums which illustrate the history of major local industries. These include *Bilston*, Staffordshire (iron and steel industry: Public Library, Museum and Art Gallery, Mount Pleasant); *Blackburn*, Lancashire (Lewis Textile Museum, Exchange Street); *Bolton*, Lancashire (Museum of Textile Machinery, Tonge Moor Road); *Clayton-le-Moors*, Lancashire (coal industry: Mercer Museum and Art Gallery, Mercer Park); *Dundee* (textiles: City Museum and Art Gallery, Albert Square); *Great Yarmouth*, Norfolk (Maritime Museum for East Anglia, Marine Parade); *Greenock*, Scotland (ports and sea-transport: McLean Museum, Union Street); *Hawick*, Scotland (knitting machinery: Wilton Lodge Museum); *High Wycombe*, Buckinghamshire (chair-making: Museum and Art Gallery, Castle Hill, Priory Avenue); *Hull*, Yorkshire (Maritime Museum, Pickering Park, Hessle Road); *Leicester* (history of technology in the East Midlands: Museum and Art Gallery, New Walk); *Northampton* (shoe-making: Central Museum, Guildhall Road).

The Waterways Museum at *Stoke Bruerne*, near Towcester in North-amptonshire, preserves barges and other material connected with canal transport. The Welsh Folk Museum at *St Fagan's Castle*, Cardiff, has mills and workshops transferred from their original sites. A regional open-air museum, covering all aspects of industry in the North-East, is now being established at *Beamish*, Co. Durham.

Many industrial firms maintain museums which are open to the public.

The finest is undoubtedly Pilkington's, at *St Helens* in Lancashire, which is devoted to glass-making. Other important collections are at TMM Research in *Helmshore*, Lancashire (early textile machines), Ruston and Hornsby in *Lincoln* (stationary engines), Steel Company of Wales in *Llanelli* (tinplate), Ferranti in *Manchester* (electrical engineering), and C. & J. Clark in *Street*, Somerset (footwear).

IRON INDUSTRY

The on-site evidence of early mining and iron-working in Britain has been very inadequately preserved. At *Coalbrookdale*, near Wellington, in Shropshire the eighteenth century furnaces where Abraham Darby pioneered the smelting of iron with coke were excavated in 1959 and opened as a museum (see plate 42). Darby converted an old (1638) charcoal blast furnace for the purpose and used the local coal, which had a low sulphur-content. This part of Shropshire, adjacent to the Severn gorge, is one of the most famous of Britain's older industrial areas. It is now scheduled as a museum complex, and includes the world's first iron bridge (1779), still spanning the Severn, which was in regular use by vehicles until 1934 (see plates 6, 7). It has a 30-metre span and a height of 11.8 metres. The parts for the bridge were cast at Coalbrookdale, which involved enlarging the original furnace, so that the great 5-ton ribs of the bridge could be cast from it. The enlarged furnace survives beneath the great dam that still blocks the furnace pool fed by the Coal Brook.

Other products of this famous foundry included cast iron cylinders for Newcomen steam engines (1723), the world's first iron rails (1767), the first iron boat (1787) and the frames for the first iron-framed building (1797). Eighteenth century mill owners were greatly plagued by fires. To counter this hazard, in 1791, the Derbyshire cotton-manufacturer, William Strutt, began building mills at *Belper* with cast iron, instead of wooden columns, but still used wooden beams. Charles Bage, of Shrewsbury, eliminated timber altogether, by using cast iron beams and columns, carrying shallow brick-vaulting, in the flax-spinning mill built for Benyon, Bage and Marshall on the northern outskirts of *Shrewsbury*. This five-storey brick building survives as Jones's Maltings, the first iron-framed structure in the world.

The best-preserved charcoal ironworks in Britain (1795) is at *Bonawe* near Taynuilt, in Argyllshire. In addition to the furnace and the charcoal store, the workers' houses and the jetty on Loch Etive, for fetching in ore and taking away pig-iron, are still to be seen. Other early Scottish ironworks, where buildings or parts of buildings still survive, are at *Wilsontown*, north of Lanark (1781), at *Muirkirk*, Kyle (1782), and *Glenbuck*, north-east of Muirkirk (1790).

COAL INDUSTRY

One of the oldest continuously worked coalmines in Britain is at *Brora*, in East Sutherland, where mining has been carried on since 1601. Production was increased in the early nineteenth century, with the development of an important local salt industry, and the present shaft dates from that time. The pit-head gear is of the old nineteenth-century type. In 1961 the pit was bought by the miners, who now work it on their own behalf.

TIN MINING AND CHINA CLAY

The Cornish tin-mining industry is now carried on at only two places, but the landscape of West Cornwall contains many examples of the buildings, now mostly ruined, which at one time housed the famous Cornish beam engines. These drained the mines and provided power for haulage. Some of these old engines have been restored and preserved, among them the rotative beam winding engine at the Levant Mine, near *St Just*, the oldest of the remaining engines in Cornwall, which was built by Harveys of Hayle in 1840 and continued working until 1930. Another engine at *Carpalla*, near St Austell, built by Harveys in 1863, worked first at West Polbreen Mine and then at Thomas' Shaft, West Kirkby Mine, St Austell. When tin-mining slumped, it was moved again, this time to a china-clay pit at Carpalla, on the main road from Newquay to St Austell, where it worked until 1942. Waterwheels were also used for pumping purposes in the china-clay industry. One survives at *Blisland*. It is 14.8 metres in diameter, and is the largest waterwheel outside the Isle of Man. It worked flat iron rods over a distance of 2.4 kilometres to pump water from a claypit.

WATERWHEELS AND WATERMILLS

The largest waterwheel of the British Isles, and in Europe, is the Great Laxey Wheel, in the Isle of Man, which was built in 1854, and has a diameter of 22 metres. It was christened Lady Isabella, in honour of the wife of the Governor of the Island. The Isle of Man is rich in metallic ores, but has no coal, so to operate the mines water power was widely used. Many of the Isle of Man wheels were 10–15 metres in diameter, but the Lady Isabella outdistanced them all. The line of pumping rods from the wheel to the top of the pit measures 182 metres, and the rods are of solid oak, strapped with plates of wrought iron. The economic depression of 1929 closed the mines and the wheel deteriorated through lack of use, until it was eventually bought and restored by a local builder.

Water-power has been of considerable importance in England, despite the great reserves of coal, and a wide range of industries depended on it, even after steam engines became reliable and relatively cheap. The eighteenth-century Arkwright Cotton Mills at *Cromford*, Derbyshire, were the first successful water-powered textile mills in the world. Arkwright built these mills, in 1771, 1777 and 1780, and parts of all three still survive. Two are side-by-side in a small valley cut by the Bonsall Brook, a tributary of the Derwent, and the third, known as Masson Mill, is by the Derwent itself, between Matlock Bridge and Cromford Bridge. All are still in use, although only Masson continues its connection with the cotton industry.

The Stott Park Bobbin Mill, at *Newby Bridge*, carries on one of the Lake District's few traditional industries, making wooden bobbins for the cotton and woollen mills. For some years after the mill was established in 1875 power was obtained from a waterwheel. Then in 1880 a steam engine was installed and the premises were extended, and worked until 1946, when electricity took over. Both the steam engine and the original mill-race are still there.

Sarehole Mill, five miles S.E. of Birmingham, at the junction of the roads coming from Wake Green and Cole Bank, was originally a cornmill. Matthew Boulton took a lease on it in 1775 and converted it to manufacture buckles and other small metal items, but gave it up in 1761, when his new factory at Soho, Birmingham, was ready. The next occupants enlarged the mill, added a second wheel and used it for blade-grinding. It reverted to cornmilling in the mid-nineteenth century and closed finally in 1919. Sarehole is one of the very few industrial survivals of the pre-steam age in Birmingham and has been restored as an important monument.

Two interesting early monuments of the Sheffield iron and steel industry have also been preserved, both of which used water-power. One is the *Abbeydale Forge* three miles from Sheffield on the Baslow road. Abbeydale began working in the 1780s and produced scythes and hay-knives. There are two waterdriven tilt-hammers and an early Huntsman crucible-steel furnace. A group of workmen's cottages has also survived and has been restored, together with the works. Shepherd Wheel, at *Whiteley Woods*, Sheffield was restored in 1962, but ended its active life in the 1930s. The waterwheel drove a number of grindstones, which were sub-contracted, grindstone by grindstone, by the main tenant to a group of workmen.

Finch Brothers' Foundry at *Sticklepath*, Devon, was, despite its name, a forge, not a foundry. Originally a clothmill, it was famous for more than a hundred years, from the 1850s onwards, for agricultural edge-tools, shovels and ladle-scoops for the china-clay industry. It has three waterwheels; one drove a pair of hammers, another a fan to provide a blast for the forges, and a third the grinding-wheel. The foundry fell into decay after closing in the late 1950s, but has now been re-roofed and preservation work has begun. Another recently restored waterdriven works is the Flint Mill, at *Cheddleton*, in North Staffordshire. In the mid-eighteenth century potters began adding flint to the clay in order to improve the whiteness of the product. The flints were first burnt in kilns and then ground to a powder with water in a pan-mill. There were many such mills in the area of the Potteries, but Cheddleton is now the only survivor in working order.

The Gunpowder Mills at *Faversham* in Kent, once the Royal Gunpowder Mills, were also waterdriven. Mills were established here as early as 1558 and Faversham is quite possibly the birthplace of Britain's gunpowder industry. The world's first gun-cotton factory was also here (1846). The mill-complex closed down in 1934, stripped of equipment and largely demolished. Chart Mills, however, were left intact and are now being restored. They consist of two pairs of mills, each working independently off a single shaft.

STEAM ENGINES

Apart from those used in connexion with mining, a number of eighteenth- and nineteenth-century steam engines have been preserved on their original sites. The earliest of these is the *Elsecar* engine (probably 1787), a Newcomen-type colliery pumping engine near Barnsley, in Yorkshire. Five of the original six beam engines, built at various dates between 1801 and 1850, have been preserved at *Kew Bridge* pumping station, which is now the museum of the Metropolitan Water Board. Two beam engines, one a Boulton and Watt of 1801, the other of 1810, are at *Crofton* pumping station, on the Kennet and Avon Canal, near Marlborough. They were in use until 1950 for lifting water to the summit of the canal.

The Dorothea slate quarries at *Tal-y-san*, near Caernarvon has the only surviving Cornish engine in Wales. Installed in 1904, with a 68-in. diameter cylinder, it was one of the last big engines to be built, and continued working until 1958.

TRANSPORT Waterways

The number of early transport monuments in Britain is so large that one can do little more than provide an arbitrary selection. Among canals, the *Exeter Canal* was one of the earliest and certainly the first to have a genuine pound lock. It was originally built in the 1560s and was extended three times, in the 1670s, in 1700 and in 1824. *Grimsby* Dock Tower (1850) is one of the most celebrated coastal monuments in Britain; it is 95 metres high

– the tallest building in Lincolnshire – and is built of brick. Originally designed as a water-accumulator for working the lock-gates and cranes, and for providing fresh water for ships, it has a tank 60 metres up the tower. The only use that can be found for it nowadays is to carry a tele-vision relay station. Another famous, and still working, hydraulic system is at Tower Bridge, in *London*. The bridge, built in 1886–94, has two bascule leaves, the power for lifting and lowering them coming from two 360-hp steam engines (1894) and a reserve 250-hp engine (1941), pumping into an accumulator.

TRANSPORT Bridges

An early suspension bridge is that at *Conway* (1822). Designed by Telford, it has stone turrets to support the chains, which are original. When a new road bridge was opened in 1958, Telford's bridge lost its income from tolls and, after a successful campaign to prevent demolition, was taken over by the National Trust. Another of Telford's designs, the *Menai* suspension bridge (1820–6) has a 176-metre span. This was reconstructed in 1940, Telford's being the road bridge. The railway over the Menai straits is carried by the Britannia bridge (1849). It was built to the design of Robert Stephenson and William Fairbairn and consists of twin wrought iron tubes, through which the trains run. The bridge was severely damaged by fire in 1970. The two spans over the water are each of 139.8 metres. A similarly impressive achievement is I. K. Brunel's Royal Albert bridge over the Tamar at *Saltash*. Built in 1858, it uses two lenticular trusses, each involving a wrought iron tube. The total length is 667.4 metres, the distance between the piers is 133 metres, and the roadway is 30 metres above high water.

TRANSPORT Railways

Other Brunel railway survivals are the two pumping-engine houses of the ill-fated atmospheric railway (1848) which ran between Exeter and Newton Abbot in Devon. The engine-house at *Starcross* is now a youth club and that at Torre is used by the Torbay Cash and Carry Company.

An early round engine-shed (1847), designed in the office of Robert Stephenson, is at Chalk Farm Road, in *London*. After the railway discarded it, it became first a wine-store and then an Arts Centre.

Among the larger nineteenth-century railway stations which have sur-vived more or less intact are those at Darlington North (1842), Paddington (1850–54), York (1873–77) and St Pancras (1875). Darlington North has a strong period flavour about it. The wide train-shed is split into two uneven halves by an iron colonnade; the roof has a massive timber frame-work. East of the station is Ignatius Bonomi's railway bridge, the oldest public railway bridge in the world. The southern part is original, the northern a later widening. Paddington was designed jointly by Brunel and Matthew Digby Wyatt. Wyatt was responsible for the buildings, Brunel for the great train-shed, which, with the disappearance of the Crystal Palace, is now the outstanding example of early iron architecture. When York was completed it was the largest station in the world. St Pancras was another example of collaboration between two architects, the splendidly engineered train-shed being by W. H. Barlow and the buildings, a notable monument of the Gothic revival, by Sir Gilbert Scott.

TRANSPORT Air

Two of the largest transport monuments in Britain are the airship hangars at *Cardington*, in Bedfordshire. The first was built in 1917 and was extended from 32.8 metres to 47.5 metres in 1927, at the time of the construction of the R.100 and R.101. A second hangar, also of 47.5 metres, was added in 1927, the year of the R.101's maiden flight.

INDUSTRIAL HOUSING

There are many survivals of early industrial housing. The best-known example is probably at *New Lanark*, in Scotland. The first mill here was built in 1785, and in 1799 the enterprise was sold to Robert Owen, who transformed it into an industrial community, with a school, meeting hall and blocks of houses. The houses were modernised in 1963, but in 1968 the owners of the business and the property, the Gourock Ropework Company, felt unable to continue and the mill is now empty. *Cronkbourne Village*, Kirk Braddon, Isle of Man, dates from 1846–50. The estate of 42 houses, in two parallel terraces, was built for the workers in the local sail-cloth factory, and it was the first community in the island to have electric light. The mill is now a laundry and the houses have been modernised. Another mid-nineteenth century estate which is being modernised is the Railway Village at *Swindon*, built in the 1840s to house employees of the Railway Works.

To illustrate further examples of the wide range of important industrial monuments which have been preserved in Britain by local and private enterprise, we may instance a brewery, a glass-works and a boathouse. The brewery is Whitbread's (late eighteenth century) in Chiswell Street, *London*. Much of this famous brewery is shortly to be demolished, but it is intended to preserve the Porter Tun Room (1773). The timber roof of this room has a clear span of 19 metres and is second only to that in Westminster Hall. *Catcliffe Glass Cone* (1740), east of Sheffield, is the earliest surviving example of a glasshouse cone. Similar examples, dating from 1825 to 1850, are to be seen in the Weser district of Germany. The boathouse (1861) is at *Sheerness Naval Dockyard*. It has a cast-iron frame and is of great architectural importance as a precursor of many modern frame-and-fill buildings.

Location of sites - England, Scotland and Wales*

Site	Lat	Long	Map	Grid
Abbeydale, south-west of Sheffield	53.20N	1.30W	Map 24	3489
Belper	53.01N	1.29W	Map 24	3445
Blisland	50.33N	4.42W	Map 4	1278
Bonawe	56.26N	5.14W	Map 51	0134
Britannia Bridge	53.14N	4.10W	Map 22	5678
Brora	58.01N	3.51W	Map 59	9001
Cardington, south-east of Bedford	52.06N	0.25W	Map 19	1245
Carpalla, east of St Stephen	50.22N	4.50W	Map 4	9056
Catcliffe	53.22N	1.21W	Map 37	4589
Chalk Farm	51.30N	0.05W	Map 13	2389
Cheddleton	53.04N	2.02W	Map 24	0156
Chiswell Street, London	51.30N	0.05W	Map 13	3489
Coalbrookdale	52.38N	2.30W	Map 23	6701
Conway	53.17N	3.50W	Map 32	7878
Crofton, south-west of Hungerford	51.23N	1.37W	Map 9	3467
Cromford	53.06N	1.34W	Map 24	3456
Cronkbourne Village, Kirk Braddon, north-west of Douglas, Isle of Man	54.09N	4.29W	Map 38	3478
Darlington	54.31N	1.34W	Map 40	2312
Elsecar, east of Hoyland Nether	53.30N	1.24W	Map 37	0134
Exeter Canal	50.43N	3.31W	Map 6	8990

Faversham	51.50N	0.53E	Map 11	0167
Glenbuck	55.33N	4.00W	Map 44	7823
Grimsby	53.35N	0.05W	Map 35	2312
Ironbridge	52.40N	2.32W	Map 23	6701
Kew Bridge	51.29N	0.18W	Map 12	1278
Laxey	54.14N	4.24W	Map 38	4589
Menai Bridge	53.14N	4.10W	Map 22	5678
Muirkirk	55.31N	4.04W	Map 44	6723
Newby Bridge	54.16N	2.58W	Map 30	3489
New Lanark	55.40N	38.48W	Map 44	8945
Paddington	51.30N	0.05W	Map 13	2389
Saltash	50.24N	4.12W	Map 5	4556
Sarehole Mill, south-east of Birmingham	52.25N	1.45W	Map 17	0178
Sheerness	51.27N	0.45E	Map 11	1078
Shepherd Wheel, Whiteley Woods, south-west of Birmingham	52.23N	1.30W	Map 24	3489
Shrewsbury	52.43N	2.45W	Map 23	4512
Starcross	50.38N	3.27W	Map 7	9089
Sticklepath	50.43N	3.56W	Map 5	6790
St Just	50.07N	5.41W	Map 4	3434
St Pancras	51.30N	0.05W	Map 13	2389
Swindon	51.34N	1.47W	Map 8	1289
Tal-y-san, east of Pen-y-groes	53.03N	4.15W	Map 22	4556
Tower Bridge	51.30N	0.05W	Map 13	3489
Wilsontown	55.47N	3.41W	Map 45	0156
York	53.58N	1.05W	Map 34	6756

* *A.A. Members Handbook, 1970–1*

BRITISH ISLES
Ireland

Ireland, taken as a whole, is very sparsely populated. The total area is 32,524 square miles and the population in 1966 was 2,884,002, of which 1,484,770 lived in the Six Counties (Ulster). A high proportion of both people and industry is concentrated in three cities, Dublin (595,288), Belfast (443,671) and Cork (120,000). The rest of Ireland is a country of small towns, where industrial development has been slow and where the population has remained almost stationary for a century, in those places where it has not actually declined.

A study of the economics of the Republic and of Ulster reveals important differences. South of the border the main industrial producers are concerned with food and drink. In the North, employment opportunities are much more balanced, with a greater emphasis on various kinds of engineering. Both Ulster and the Republic are, however, very short of science-based industries and consequently find it difficult to provide adequate opportunities for highly trained scientists and technologists. Since 1945, however, both countries have made great efforts to expand and modernise their industries and this has necessarily involved an acceleration in the policy of scrapping and replacing old buildings and machinery.

MUSEUMS

Ireland is not rich in museums, either public or private. The Ulster Museum at Stranmillis in *Belfast* has a large department devoted to technology and local history, and the Ulster Folk Museum at Cultra Manor, *Holywood*, has a number of exhibits relating to small-scale industries. There is a Transport Museum, also in Belfast, in Witham Street.

31

There is no publicly-run museum in the Republic which specialises in the history of science or technology, although the National Museum of Ireland, Kildare Street, *Dublin* has a few relevant exhibits in its Art and Industrial Division. Folk museums have been established at The Castle, *Enniscorthy*, and at *Killarney*, and, very recently, a Steam Preservation Museum at *Stradbally*.

The only company museum of any note belongs to Guinness, the great Dublin brewery firm. The first Arthur Guinness began brewing at *St James's Gate*, in 1759, but the idea of preserving any of the relics of the firm's development was not officially accepted until the Bicentenary of 1959 approached. The Museum, in the old research laboratory building, was opened in 1968. The theme of the collection is gradually broadening out to cover Irish brewing and distilling in general.

BREWING

The brewery at *Kilkenny* was established before Guinness began in Dublin. Among the many breweries in Kilkenny during the eighteenth century was Sullivans, which was bought by Smithwicks in 1819. An archway in this brewery, subsequently used as a maltings, is inscribed 'IA 1702 D. James Sullivan'. The present main brewery was built by Edmund Smithwick (1800–76). There is a waterwheel (1817) which used to drive the brewhouse machinery and a D.C. generator, and nearby is a beam engine (*c.* 1860) which was brought into service in times of drought and flood. The business was bought by Guinness in 1964 and a new brewhouse has since been built.

It is probable that there are other beam engines still surviving in the Republic's many distilleries. Distilleries, however, are notoriously difficult to enter, and so a proper record of Irish beam engines is still to be made.

TRANSPORT   Railways

The Irish railways have been drastically pruned in the post-war years, and little capital has been made available for rebuilding stations. In general, however, the stations in the Republic are distinguished more for their names than for their architecture. In *Dublin*, heroes of the Civil War are commemorated at Pearse, Connolly and Heuston Stations, and in the west Tralee Casement carries on the same tradition. Of the main stations in Dublin, Kingsbridge and Broadstone, both dating from the 1870s, are the most interesting.

One of the most remarkable railway stations in Ireland is at *Helen's Bay*, Co. Down (see plate 20), built in the Scottish baronial style to the requirements of the Marquis of Dufferin and Ava, by the Belfast, Holywood and Bangor Railway, which extended the line from Holywood to Bangor in 1865. There was a private waiting room for the Marquis and his family, and between the gables is a panel bearing the Dufferin and Ava initials, surmounted by a coronet. Another example of pressure by landed interests on the railway company is the single-tracked tunnel, half a mile long, at *Dungannon*, Co. Tyrone, which is now abandoned. This took the line out of its way in order to avoid spoiling the view from a country house. The oldest station in Ulster is at *Moira*, Co. Antrim, which was built in 1841–42, when the line of the Ulster Railway was extended from Lisburn to Lurgan.

A few of the red sandstone railway bridges remain between Belfast and Lisburn, built 1837–39 on the original section of the Ulster Railway. At *Craigmore*, near Bessbrook, Co. Armagh, there is an impressive 18-arch viaduct of 1851–52 which carries the main Dublin–Belfast line.

The main railway workshops in the Republic are at *Dundalk*, where locomotives have been built and repaired for more than 120 years. Dundalk is also the centre of an old-established boot and shoe industry; the older buildings at Halliday's factory date from the 1880s.

TRANSPORT Waterways

In the Republic there is only one canal system of any consequence, the Grand Canal (1772–1830), running across Ireland from Dublin in the East to Limerick and Ballinasloe in the West. There were branches to Naas, Kilbeggan, Edenderry, Maintmellick, and via the Barrow navigation to Waterford, giving a total of 557 kilometres of inland waterways. The Canal Harbour at St James's Street, Dublin, was extensively used by Guinness's Brewery. Smeaton was consultant to the British Government in connection with the building of this canal. There are two much shorter canals, the Royal in Dublin and the Corrib which provided a link between Lough Corrib and Galway Bay.

The most elaborate inland waterway system in Northern Ireland is around Lough Neagh. The Irish Parliament voted large sums for the construction of a canal to *Newry* in the mistaken belief that there were extensive deposits of coal on the Tyrone shore of the lake. The Newry Navigation was completed in 1744, and was the first work of its kind in the British Isles. The port of Newry was further improved by the building of a ship canal in 1759–65. The River Lagan was made navigable as far as Lisburn in 1759–63, but the canal between the river and Lough Neagh was not completed until 1796. However, these canals with their many locks were far too ambitious for the capital resources of eighteenth-century Ireland, and there was no bulky traffic to make them profitable.

Near *Coalisland*, Co. Tyrone, there are the remains of a gravitational incline or 'dry hurry', on the former tub-boat canal and not far away, at *Newmills* there is a canal aqueduct dating from 1770.

The Lower Bann Navigation has a double lock and dry dock at *Portna*, Co. Londonderry, and on the Lower Bann itself, at The Cutts, near *Coleraine* there is a curious but pleasant combination of lock, fishery, floodgate and rapid.

TRANSPORT   Harbour and Docks

At the height of its prosperity, *Kinsale*, Co. Cork, was one of the chief ports of the British Navy, but its docks and quays were too small to accommodate the bigger ships of the later eighteenth century or the expansion of the shipbuilding industry during the same period. The harbour and a few surrounding small warehouses bear witness to the town's former maritime importance. Other pleasant eighteenth- and early nineteenth-century warehouses in varying stages of decay, are to be seen at *Waterford* and *Limerick*.

Early in the nineteenth century *Dun Laoghaire* was a small fishing village. Its importance grew rapidly after the railway to Dublin was opened in 1834, a new harbour was completed in 1859 and Dun Laoghaire became the Irish terminus of the mailboat service to Holyhead. The railway station (1837) is one of the earliest in the British Isles. A former mail packet harbour, designed by Rennie, is at *Donaghadee*, Co. Down.

The shipbuilding industry in *Belfast* on the Lagan was founded by William and Hugh Ritchie in 1791, and later Harland and Wolff established their great concern here in 1862.

COAL MINING

Ireland has one or two areas where coal-mining is carried on, although on a modest scale. The Leinster Coalfield, the most important, produces anthracite, and has surface installations dating back about a hundred years. The main town here is *Castlecomer*, Co. Kilkenny. In the nineteenth century, both coal and iron were mined in the *Arigna Mountains*, near Lough Allen, Co. Leitrim. Coal is still worked there under rather primitive conditions, but the extraction of the iron-ore is no longer found profitable. Coal is also worked in the South, but here too the scale of operations is not large.

The coal deposits at *Coalisland*, Co. Tyrone, were worked intermittently for nearly 200 years, until production finally ceased in the 1930s. Coalisland had several industries – fireclay, bricks, linen-weaving, corn and flour milling – in the eighteenth century, and buildings belonging to all of them still survive.

COPPER, GOLD AND LEAD MINING

At *Avoca*, in Co. Wicklow, there are deposits of pyrites, containing ores of copper, lead, zinc, and sulphur. These were known in Roman times and were worked until recently and the old workings and parts of smelters are still in evidence. Here, as in the other copper-mining districts of Co. Cork and Co. Waterford, there are the ruined engine houses of the former pumping engines.

Woodenbridge, Co. Wicklow, has gold-mining associations. The goldsmiths of ancient Ireland obtained much of their gold from Croghan Kinsella, at the head of the Gold Mines River, a few miles south-west of Woodenbridge. In 1796 the discovery of a nugget there led to a gold rush and in a few months 2,600 ounces were found.

What might perhaps be described as a negative industrial monument exists at *Newtownhamilton*, Co. Armagh. This was once a heavily forested area, but the timber was cut down during the eighteenth century to provide fuel for a lead-smelting works. The lead workings were shallow and the site can still be distinguished by the disturbed ground.

WINDMILLS

Very few Irish windmills survive in anything like complete condition. One that does is at *Teceenslane*, Co. Wexford, which is preserved as a national monument. There is an extraordinary density of windmill sites around Strangford Lough near Belfast, especially in the Ards Peninsula. The only complete mill is at *Ballycopeland*, Co. Down. It ceased working in 1915, but has been preserved as a state monument, and was extensively repaired in 1958–59.

TEXTILES

The valleys of the Upper Bann and Lagan and the adjoining districts of the counties of Antrim, Armagh, and Down have been the heart of the Irish linen industry since the late seventeenth century, and the area has many monuments of the cotton and linen industries. Waterpower was widely used for washing and pounding the cloth after about 1730. After the cotton industry had been introduced into the Belfast area in the last quarter of the eighteenth century, large-scale spinning and weaving mills began to spread to the production of linen cloth as well, although weaving was mechanised much later than spinning.

One of the oldest flax spinning mills is at *Coose*, Co. Down. Dating from the 1830s, it belongs to the Hazelbank Weaving Company and is in an excellent state of preservation. The threadwork of Dunbar McMaster and Company at *Loughans* is the largest industrial undertaking on the Upper Bann; the present buildings all date from the second half of the nineteenth century. John Andrews' spinning mill at *Comber* was built in 1863 and is a fine example of mill architecture.

The disused barracks at *Newry*, Co. Down, was originally built as a white-linen hall for the town of Newry. The walled area encloses over six acres. The hall was built in 1783 to develop the export of linen from the north of Ireland, without using the Dublin merchants. It proved to be a serious misjudgement, partly because the new Belfast white-linen hall made Newry's unnecessary, and partly because the bleachers preferred to deal direct with their customers in Britain.

Location of sites - Ireland*

Arigna mountains, north of Drumshanbo	52.49N	7.56W	Map 11	9012
Avoca	52.52N	6.13W	Map 9	1290
Ballycopeland	54.40N	5.35W	Map 15	5678
Belfast	54.35N	5.55W	Map 15	3478
Castlecomer	52.48N	7.14W	Map 8	5678
Coalisland	54.33N	6.42W	Map 14	8967
Coleraine	55.08N	6.40W	Map 14	8934
Comber	54.33N	5.45W	Map 15	4578
Coose, west of Banridge	52.24N	5.54W	Map 15	1245
Craigmore, north-west of Newry	54.12N	6.20W	Map 13	0123
Donaghadee	54.39N	5.33W	Map 15	5689
Dublin	53.20N	6.15W	Map 9	1234
Dundalk	54.01N	6.25W	Map 13	0101
Dungannon, Co. Tyrone	54.31N	6.46W	Map 14	8967
Dun Laoghaire	53.17N	6.08W	Map 9	2323
Galway (Lough Corrib)	53.16N	9.03W	Map 6	2323
Helen's Bay	54.40N	5.49W	Map 15	4589

Kilkenny	52.39N	7.15w	Map	5 5656
Kinsale	51.40N	8.30w	Map	3 6756
Limerick	52.40N	8.38w	Map	7 5656
Loughans	54.40N	6.29w	Map	15 0990
Moira	54.29N	6.14w	Map	15 1267
Newmills, south-east of Coalisland	54.32N	6.41w	Map	14 8967
Newry	54.11N	6.20w	Map	13 0123
Newtownhamilton	54.12N	6.35w	Map	13 9023
Portna	55.05N	6.38w	Map	15 0101
Teceenslane	52.30N	6.16w	Map	5 1223
Waterford	52.15N	7.06w	Map	5 6712
Woodenbridge	52.50N	6.13w	Map	9 1278

* *A.A. Handbook, Ireland, 1970–71*

BULGARIA

Although Bulgaria achieved its own government in 1878, it was not completely independent of Turkey until 1908. In 1878, Bulgaria was an exceedingly backward nation, both economically and culturally. Agriculture and stockbreeding constituted the two main sectors of the economy and even these were primitive in organisation and character. Industry, so far as it existed at all, was on a domestic and handicraft workshop scale. A survey carried out when the new government was set up in 1878 showed that Bulgaria possessed only 20 enterprises which could be described as factories. Of these, ten belonged to the food and beverage industry, four to textiles, five to leather and fur and one to metal-working; there was no heavy industry of any kind.

The new state attempted to develop industry by introducing high tariffs on imports and by a series of laws to encourage and protect home industry, which included the 1894 Law for the Compulsory Wearing of Home-Made Clothes and Shoes. These measures produced some results, but even at the outbreak of war in 1914, the level of industrialisation was still very low. Estimates made at that time showed that manufacturing fell into three categories. Goods produced actually in people's homes accounted for 26 per cent. of the total, artisan workshops added a further 50 per cent. and factories were responsible for the remaining 24 per cent. The most notable increase had been in ceramics, which was probably due to the urban construction of public buildings and blocks of flats, all needing kitchen and sanitary facilities.

The two World Wars did little but harm to the Bulgarian economy. In particular, the number of craftsmen working on their own or with one or two assistants was considerably higher in 1945 than it had been in 1920. If one takes stock of the economy at the peak of its capitalist period, 1939, one can see that advances had been made in coal mining, the metal industries and textiles, but that capital goods formed under a quarter of the total output. Bulgarian industry was small-scale and lop-sided, and technically very backward. Much of it was under foreign control; in 1938, 31 enterprises with foreign capital accounted for 32 per cent. of the value of the total industrial output. This was especially marked in the production of cement, electric power, matches, paper, mining, salt, textiles, tobacco, brewing and flour milling. In 1939, the foreign capital was mainly German.

Since 1945 all industry has been socialised and the present distribution, variety and size of plants bears little relation to the pre-war pattern. One could perhaps summarise the position now, in 1971, by saying that nearly every manifestation of industry which one sees in Bulgaria today is no more than 25 years old. To all intents and purposes, industrial archaeology in Bulgaria began in 1945. The industrial history of Britain, France or Germany covers a period of more than two centuries, while the main industrial development of Bulgaria has been compressed into a quarter of a century, and one has to adjust one's time-scale and targets of observation accordingly.

MUSEUMS

All the main towns of Bulgaria have what is described as a Town Historical Museum. These museums all put a heavy emphasis on the achievements of the past 25 years and provide a somewhat simplified interpretation of the economic and social history of the district during the previous hundred years. They are, however, very useful in the way in which they add detail and local colour to the generalised statements given in the first four paragraphs of the present section. More ambitious historical museums are to be found at *Dimitrovgrad* (Museum of Socialist Construction), *Pernik* (Museum of the Revolutionary Movement and Socialist Construction, Kracho Selo Quarter, Block 8), and *Plovdiv* (Museum of the Revolutionary Movement of Socialist Construction).

There are two open-air museums, both with material illustrating the old small-scale methods of manufacture and milling. One is at *Etura*, the open-air Ethnographical Museum, and the other, much larger, at *Kazanlük*, the Shipka-Bouzloudía National Park Museum. *Ruse* has a Museum of Transport and *Varna* a Naval Museum, while the main museum devoted to agricultural history is in *Sofia*.

COAL AND METAL MINING

Two major coal-mining regions have been developed since 1945, one in the south which includes the *Pernik* coal basin, and one in the south-east, covering the *Maritsa-East* and *Maritsa-West* basins.

The only iron-producing area includes the *Kremikovtsi* iron-ore deposits and the Pernik coal basin. There are two regions which produce non-ferrous metals – around *Kŭrdzhali*, *Smolyan* and *Plovdiv* in the south, which has lead and zinc ores, and around *Sofia* and *Vratsa* in the west, which specialises in the production of copper and rare metals. Machine-building and metal processing are scattered all over the country, with concentrations at *Sofia*, *Varna*, *Ruse*, *Burgas* and *Plovdiv*.

CHEMICALS, RUBBER AND TEXTILES

The chemical and rubber industry is concentrated mainly in the areas of *Sofia*, *Dimitrovgrad*, *Varna*, *Reka Devnya* and *Plovdiv*. The major centres of the textile industry are *Plovdiv*, *Varna*, *Vratsa*, *Sliven*, *Sofia* and *Gabrovo*.

FOOD PRODUCTION

The food and drink industries are widely scattered, but three main concentrations can be distinguished. The first, in South Bulgaria, is primarily concerned with canning and tobacco manufacture. It includes the towns of *Plovdiv*, *Pazardzhik*, *Asenovgrad* and *Pŭrvomay*. The second, in the north of the country, specialises in canning, sugar refining and meat processing, and is based on *Gorna Oryakhovitsa*, *Veliko Tŭrnovo* and *Lyaskovets*. The third region, also in North Bulgaria, has *Pleven* and *Cherven Brijag* as its chief centres, and produces flour, canned goods, processed poultry, vegetable oils and sugar.

WINE INDUSTRY

An interesting feature of the modern post-war economy of Bulgaria is its large-scale wine industry. Big vineyards, laid out to permit the maximum use of machinery, are grouped around factory-type processing plants, capable of dealing with up to 1,200 tons of grapes in 24 hours. Examples of these fully mechanised plants can be seen at *Sofia*, *Ruse* and *Pleven*, while very good champagne is produced at the factory at *Lyaskovets* – but it is a factory in the modern sense with no antiquity, tradition or romance about it.

41

Location of sites - **Bulgaria***

Asenovgrad	42.00N 24.53E	Map	9 CD 34
Burgas	42.30N 27.29E	Map	9 EF 45
Cherven Brijag	43.17N 24.07E	Map	9 BC 45
Dimitrovgrad	42.03N 25.34E	Map	9 DE 45
Gabrovo	42.52N 25.19E	Map	9 CD 45
Gorna Oryakhovitsa	43.07N 25.40E	Map	9 DE 45
Kazanlŭk	42.37N 25.23E	Map	9 CD 45
Kremikovtsi	41.29N 25.38E	Map	9 DE 23
Kŭrdzhali	41.38N 25.21E	Map	9 CD 34
Lyaskovets	43.05N 25.42E	Map	9 DE 45
Maritsa	42.01N 25.50E	Map	9 DE 34
Pazardzhik	42.10N 24.20E	Map	9 BC 34
Pernik	42.36N 23.03E	Map	9 AB 45
Pleven	43.25N 24.40E	Map	9 CD 56
Plovdiv	42.08N 24.45E	Map	9 CD 34
Pŭrvomay	42.06N 25.14E	Map	9 CD 34
Reka Devnya	43.15N 27.3E	Map	9 EF 56
Ruse	43.50N 25.59E	Map	9 DE 56
Sliven	42.40N 26.19E	Map	9 DE 45
Smolyan	41.34N 24.42E	Map	9 CD 23
Sofia	42.40N 23.18E	Map	9 BC 45
Varna	43.12N 27.57E	Map	9 EF 56
Veliko Tŭrnovo	43.04N 25.39E	Map	9 DE 45
Vratsa	43.12N 23.32E	Map	9 BC 45

* *A.A. Eastern European Handbook, 1970–1*

CZECHOSLOVAKIA

Since 1945 the Czechs have followed a flexible, realistic policy towards their technical monuments, recognising on the one hand the importance of preserving as many of the outstanding monuments as possible and on the other the inevitability, in most cases, of some kind of compromise. At the Wallsteiner Foundry at *Starý Plzenec* for example, it proved possible to save the old furnace and the building in which it stood by converting the whole area into a factory museum, but the surrounding buildings which were contemporary with the furnace had to go, to make room for part of a programme of modernisation and expansion. Other instances, where the exterior has been preserved at the price of modernisation or replacement of the old plant, are the ironworks at *Malinec* and the paper-mill at *Velké Losiny*.

In the past, the policy has been to restore and preserve technical monuments only if they are considered to have considerable architectural merit. Many bridges have come into this category, including the medieval Karl's Bridge in *Prague* and the 1721 bridge at *Koči*, and also windmills, particularly in South and North Moravia.

MUSEUMS

The problem of dealing satisfactorily with monuments of great technical interest but relatively little architectural merit is a new one and appears to be solved best by attaching the monument to a museum as a kind of extra-mural branch.

In this way, the regional Technical Museum in *Košice* has made itself responsible for one of the last surviving hammer-iron works in Slovakia at

43

A Guide to the Industrial Archaeology of Europe

Nižni Medzev, the Museum of the Glass Industry at *Jablonec* (Nisou, Jiráskova 4) looks after the remains of an old glass-working settlement at *Kristiánov*, and the South Bohemian Museum in *České Budějovice* takes care of the last of the station buildings on the old horse-drawn railway from České Budějovice to Linz.

Czechoslovakia is a country with an exceptionally large number of local museums. Many of them contain important technical exhibits and documentation relating to them and the two National Technical Museums, one in *Prague* (Kostelní 42) and the other in *Košice*, maintain a good information service between themselves and the local centres. The National Technical Museum in Prague, which was established in 1908, is one of the oldest in Europe. There are two open-air museums, both recent, one at *Rožňava* and the other, for Slovakia, at *Martin*.

Antol has a museum for the woodworking industry and the museums at *Bratislava* (Stará Radnica), *Mikulov* and *Pezinok* contain sections dealing with the production of wine. The collections of the National Agricultural Museum in *Prague* (Slezská 7) necessarily overlap both with those of the National Technical Museums and with those of local and more specialised museums. This is especially the case for the exhibits illustrating wine growing and production and milk-processing. In *Karlovy Vary* the Municipal Museum (Zámecky urch 22) includes an industrial section, and there is a museum at the College of Mining and Metallurgy at *Ostrava* (Dvorákova 7). The famous brewery museum at *Plzeň* now forms part of the West Bohemian Museum, and is located in an old brewery.

Many of the provincial collections are now in the care of local research institutes concerned with the historical development of a particular industry. Such institutes are to be found for the mining industry at *Kutná Hora*, *Jáchymov*, *Krupka*, *Chomutov*, *Most* and *Sokolov*, for the textile industry at *Vrchlabe*, *Rychnov* and *Ústi nad Orlicí*, and for the glass industry at *Jablonec*, Kamenicky Senov, and Novy Bor.

A number of other sites, restored since 1945, may be mentioned, in order to show the activity of State and local preservation organisations.

The beautiful eighteenth-century saltworks, the Salná Baňa, at *Presov*, with its baroque clocktower and arcaded façade, has been restored and preserved. The salt boiling-house, brine-shaft, store, church and cemetery are interesting survivals of an industrial community. So, on a different scale, are the old buildings used by the wine industry at *Petrov* and *Prušankach*, near Hodonin.

Preservation of industrial monuments in Czechoslovakia covers a wide range of types and sizes of structure. The windmill which has been restored to working order at Ruprechtova, in the *Vyškov* district, is one of the most remarkable and beautiful in Europe, with its round stone tower and Greek-type sails, perched like a catherine-wheel on top of the conical roof.

IRON INDUSTRY

There are museums devoted to the iron industry at *Hořovice* and *Komárov*, which illustrate the development of the industry in their particular areas. These museums are small and a proposal has been made to set up a much larger museum for the Bohemian iron industry as a whole at *Jínce*. The old ironworks here, near *Příbram*, has a charcoal-fuelled blast-furnace dating from 1810, in good condition. Jínce is in the Brdy Forest district, which was the most important in Bohemia during the seventeenth and eighteenth centuries. Near to Jínce, is *Dobřiv*, where a nineteenth-century forge and foundry has recently been restored. This works, the Upper Works, was one of five which operated in Dobřiv in the nineteenth century, and since the works was restored in 1955 it has been in production again.

Another carefully restored monument of the iron industry is the water-driven forge at Medzeve, near *Košice*, which has an overshot wheel and a beautifully constructed wooden leat for bringing the water to it.

The iron industry in Czechoslovakia is very old. In 1700 there were 77 blast-furnaces in Bohemia and Moravia, but towards the end of the eighteenth century the timber shortage became serious and the ironworks began to abandon the production of wrought iron and to turn to cast iron, which used less fuel. In Moravia the *Adamov* ironworks was supplying munitions on a considerable scale by 1800, with an annual output of several dozen cannon and hundreds of thousands of cannon balls each year. The remains of the old blast-furnace, dating from 1752, are still to be seen there, conveniently by the side of a good road. The furnace, square-sectioned and tapering towards the top, is built of stone, with brick arches. The site is scheduled as a national monument, and is under the supervision of the Technical Museum in Brno.

The Slovak foundries, too, did well during the eighteenth century. The most important was at *Lubietová*, which was linked to the nearby ore-mines at *Banská Stiavnica* and *Banská Bystrica*. These mines were greatly helped by the Habsburg mercantilist policy and reached a high level of technical development. The first atmospheric engine in any mine outside England was installed at *Nová Baňa* in Slovakia in 1722–24.

The Czechoslovak iron-founders had a superb technique, of a much higher standard than that in England at the same period. In the early 1800s the *Komárov* ironworks was producing iron bracelets and necklaces of wonderfully high quality, and the workmanship of Komárov cast iron busts is equal to anything the bronze-founders could achieve. Their larger decorative castings, made during the first half of the nineteenth century, are to be found over a wide area. They include tomb-plates, crosses and minor statuary of all kinds, and there are some interesting branched lamp-posts in *Prague*, cast at Komárov in the 1860s. The foundry was also making cast iron bridges in the first quarter of the nineteenth century, of which two survived until the Second World War.

With the introduction of coke blast-furnaces in the middle of the last century, the use of structural iron increased enormously. In 1859 the Tyl Theatre in *Prague* was reconstructed, with 108 cast iron columns and wrought iron brackets supporting the galleries, to replace the original wooden structure of 1783. The new iron-work was produced by Ringhoffer Works in Prague, which are still in operation. One of the most elaborate pieces of nineteenth-century iron-work is the marvellous cast iron colonnade at *Marianské Lázně* (Marienbad) (see plates 47, 48), which was built by the Blansko Ironworks in 1889.

SILVER AND RADIUM MINING

A number of metals have been mined in the area of *Jáchymov* (Joachimstal). The mines were opened at the beginning of the sixteenth century and for several decades they produced a high proportion of Europe's silver. Between 1520 and 1560 a number of new mining towns were established in the area, among them *Lovčna* and *Hornt Blatná*. Similar mines were operating in *Krušné Hory* from the eighteenth century onwards. During the present century radium has been produced in steadily increasing quantities from the Jáchymov mine, and one of the earlier radium mines, *Svornost*, has been preserved as an historical site.

The Mining School at Jáchymov was founded in 1716, the earliest in Europe, and a Chair of Mining was established in Prague in 1763. A new museum has been opened at Jáchymov, illustrating the whole range of mining activity in the area. It includes the fine library of the town's old Latin School.

TRANSPORT Railways

At *České Budějovice* ceremonies took place in 1968 to celebrate the centenary of the opening of the railway between Plzen (Pilsen) and what was then called Budweis and is now České Budějovice. This provided rail links with Prague, Vienna, Bavaria and Saxony. Thirty years earlier Budweis had been the terminus of the horse-drawn railway to Linz, built between 1825 and 1832. During the centenary celebrations the proposal was made to establish a special kind of transport museum in the area, and a small historical collection is being established in the old horse-railway station in Mánesova Ulice at České Budějovice. This building belongs to the old-established Koh-I-Noor pencil factory, which itself maintains an historical museum. A stretch of the line, between *Pšenice* and *Rybnik*, is

46

being restored to show the techniques employed in building bridges, cuttings and embankments which were of great value to the later railway builders. When this is completed, the project will be one of the most imaginative and attractive pieces of railway preservation in Europe.

Location of sites - **Czechoslovakia***

Adamov, north of Chrudim	49.60N 15.50	Map	4 EF 45
Antol, near Zvolen	49.35N 19.10E	Map	5 CD 23
Banská Bystrica	48.44N 19.10E	Map	5 CD 34
Banská Stiavnica	48.29N 18.50E	Map	5 CD 23
Bratislava	48.10N 17.10E	Map	5 AB 23
České Budějovice	49.00N 17.30E	Map	4 DE 34
Chomutov	50.28N 13.25E	Map	4 DE 56
Dobřiv	49.47N 14.10E	Map	4 DE 45
Hořovice	49.50N 13.55E	Map	4 DE 45
Jablonec	50.54N 15.10E	Map	4 EF 56
Jáchymov (Joachimstal)	50.22N 12.55E	Map	4 CD 45
Jínce, north of Přibram	49.48N 13.59E	Map	4 DE 45
Karlovy Vary	50.14N 12.53E	Map	4 CD 45
Koči	50.00N 16.10E	Map	4 DE 45
Komárov, north-west of Chrudim	49.61N 15.48E	Map	4 EF 45
Košice	48.44N 21.15E	Map	5 DE 34
Kristiánov, east of Jablonec	50.54N 15.10E	Map	4 EF 56
Krupka, south-west of Zatec	50.11N 13.44E	Map	4 DE 45
Krušné Hory	50.24N 10.27E	Map	4 CD 56
Kutná Hora	49.58N 15.15E	Map	4 EF 45
Lubietová, north of Banská Bystrica	48.45N 19.08E	Map	5 CD 34
Malinec	48.32N 19.40E	Map	5 CD 23
Marianské Lázně (Marienbad)	49.59N 12.40E	Map	4 CD 45
Martin	49.05N 18.55E	Map	5 CD 34
Mikulov	48.58N 16.40E	Map	5 AB 34
Most	50.31N 13.39E	Map	4 DE 56

Nižni Medzev, west of Košice	48.43N 20.55E	Map 5	CD 23
Nová Bana	48.28N 18.40E	Map 5	BC 23
Ostrava	49.50N 18.15E	Map 5	BC 45
Petrov, north-east of Hódonin	48.55N 17.19E	Map 4	FG 34
Pezinok, north-east of Bratislava	48.17N 17.15E	Map 4	FG 23
Plzeň	49.45N 13.25E	Map 4	CD 45
Prague	49.39N 13.49E	Map 4	DE 45
Prešov	49.00N 21.10E	Map 5	DE 34
Příbram	49.42N 14.00E	Map 15	CD 56
Prušankach	48.52N 17.10E	Map 4	FG 34
Pšenice, near Rybnik	48.38N 14.27E	Map 4	DE 34
Rožňava	48.40N 20.30E	Map 4	DE 34
Rybnik, south-west of České Budějovice	48.38N 14.27E	Map 4	DE 34
Rychnov	50.10N 16.17E	Map 4	FG 45
Salná Baňa, south-east of Presov	49.00N 14.30E	Map 4	DE 34
Sokolov	50.10N 12.30E	Map 4	CD 45
Starý Plzenec, south-east of Pilsen	49.43N 13.35E	Map 4	DE 45
Svornost, south-east of Jáchymov	50.21N 12.56E	Map 4	CD 45
Ústí nad Orlicí	50.00N 16.25E	Map 4	FG 45
Velké Losiny, north of Sumperk	49.58N 17.00E	Map 4	FG 45
Vrchlabé	50.38N 15.35E	Map 4	EF 56
Vyškov	49.19N 17.00E	Map 4	DE 34

* *A.A. Eastern European Handbook, 1970–1*

DENMARK

Denmark is generally thought of as an agricultural country, and fifty years ago this was largely true; nowadays, however, only 13 per cent. of the Danish working population makes a living from agriculture, a proportion lower than that of most other Continental countries. Danish farms are highly mechanised and the concept of each farm being a one-man agricultural factory is not far from being a reality. The great majority of Danish industries are processing industries; iron, coal, metals, oil and most other raw materials have to be imported. The only large industry in Denmark, apart from food-processing, to be based on indigenous raw materials is the cement industry. Since the early nineteenth century, cement production has been associated with the manufacture of cement-making machinery, and more than a thousand of the cement factories now operating throughout the world are Danish-equipped. Denmark was one of the pioneering countries in concrete technology, and from the mid-nineteenth century onwards Danish engineers have been building roads, bridges, tunnels and harbours all over the world.

There are about 6,000 industrial firms in Denmark. The typical Danish firm employs between 25 and 200 workers, but uses advanced methods. The population, too, is small – only 5 million – but the amount of world trade per head is the highest in the world. Nowhere in Denmark is more than thirty miles from a port, and shipping and ship-building are two of the principal industries. It was a Danish yard which, in 1912, launched the world's first diesel-engined ship.

Metal-working is now the leading industry, employing nearly 40 per cent. of all industrial workers. Denmark exports over two-thirds of her agricultural production; she is the world's biggest exporter of meat and meat products, the second largest exporter of butter, and the third largest exporter of cheese. The industries allied to agriculture, such as those producing agricultural machinery, food-processing machines and pesticides, have also developed fast.

It has been of great value to Denmark that the small size of its firms has allowed an old handicraft tradition to be carried over into the industrial age. This tradition has been the basis of the lively activity which, since 1945, has given rise to the concept of Danish design, especially in furnishing and textiles.

Since so many of Denmark's industries are of very recent growth and since the country has to live on its brains and its exports, both manufacturing equipment and the buildings housing it tend to be replaced quickly, and Denmark, as a country, is one of the poorest industrial museums in the world.

MUSEUMS

The Royal Danish Porcelain Factory in *Copenhagen* can be visited, and among the other relevant museums in Denmark are the Railway Museum (Jernbanemuseet), the Agricultural Museum (Landbrugsmuseet) and the Fishing Museum (Nørregade 7 B.K.), also in Copenhagen; the Trade and Shipping Museum (Handels og Søfartsmuseet, Kronborg Castle) and the Technical Museum (Danmarks Tekniske Museum, Ndr. Strandvej 23) both in *Helsingør*. The Technical Museum is an independent institution, founded in 1911 by the Associations of Danish Industries and Handicrafts, and now receives subsidies from both the Government and from industry. During recent years a number of specialised collections have been incorporated in the Museum, including the technological collection from Denmark's Technical University, the museum belonging to the Copenhagen Telephone Company, and the Aalborg Industrial Museum.

The large museum maintained by Burmeister and Wain, the Copenhagen firm of shipbuilders and diesel-engine manufacturers is very fine. It is open to the public, but, for some reason, is not mentioned in tourist literature. Burmeister and Wain were established in 1843, and their story is closely interwoven with the career of Rudolf Diesel, whose inventions brought small profit to himself and much to Copenhagen and to Burmeister and Wain. There is an Automobile Museum at *Nysted*, Aalholm.

Denmark's agricultural history is excellently documented in the charming and well-arranged Agricultural Museum (Landbrugsmuseet, Kongevejen 100) at *Sorgenfri*, near Copenhagen. The Open Air Museum (Frilandsmuseet) at *Lyngby*, to the north of Copenhagen, has agricultural buildings, workshops and mills from all parts of Denmark. The mills transferred to Lyngby include a Greek-type vertical mill from Sandø in the

the Faroes, (1800), a watermill from Småland (1825) and the much earlier Nymølle, of 1688.

MILLS

Mills are in the special and official care of the Danish Mill Preservation Board (Nationalmuseet Mølleudvalg), a largely autonomous department of the National Museum. The enlightened policy and remarkable activity of the Danish Mill Preservation Board have made wind- and water-mills much the most most important group of industrial monuments in Denmark. The aim, wherever possible, is to restore the mill and get it working again for a useful purpose. The Danish mills are consequently living mills, not museum pieces and they contain a remarkably wide range of industries. Of a total of more than fifty mills which have been restored and preserved, we have chosen ten as representative.

Wind and water power has been of great importance in Denmark until comparatively recent years, since all coal has to be imported. The Board has its headquarters in a mill at *Brede Værk*, Lyngby (see plate 64). Brede Værk is itself an industrial monument of considerable importance. Throughout the Middle Ages waterpower was probably used on this site by the tanners for grinding bark and for softening and thinning the hides after tanning. In 1628 a gunpowder mill was installed here, then in 1668 the powder mill gave way to a copper-works. These works operated until 1810, producing copper and brass utensils and scythes. From 1810 onwards the place was gradually rebuilt as a textile factory. In 1840 came the first steam engines, and shortly afterwards the early water-turbines and power-looms. In 1908 large reinforced concrete mill-buildings were erected, which are among the earliest in Denmark. The firm, I. C. Modeweg and Sons, went out of business in 1956 and the buildings were bought by the Government, as a store and workshops for the National Museum.

On the same river, the Mølleaa (the Mill river), are two mills at *Lyngby* known as the Northern and the Southern Mill. The Northern Mill was built in 1600, and until the early eighteenth century was used mainly as a mill for fulling cloth, but later turned to grinding corn. Plans are under way to restore and return it to active life as a corn mill. The Southern Mill, always a cereal mill, was much older, but it was burnt down in 1902 and rebuilt as a modern turbine mill, which is still working.

Ørholm Mill, also on the Mølleaa, began producing gunpowder in the seventeenth century. During the eighteenth it turned successively to starch, iron and copper, scythes, and cutlery, and between 1794 and 1933 it was a papermill. The mills are now used for other industrial purposes, not using waterpower. The last turbine used by the papermills, an 1872

Fourneyron up-flow turbine, produced by Nagel and Kemp in Hamburg and cast by the Lüneburger Eisenwerk, has been given to the National Museum at Brede and is to be re-installed there.

Strandmøllen, on the coastal road from Copenhagen to Helsingør, is one of the oldest mills along the Mølleaa. This short stretch of river is known to have had nine mills on it. There was a papermill, the largest in Denmark, where paper-making lasted until the First World War. There was also a cornmill early in the seventeenth century but the mill now produces oxygen and other gases.

Børkop Mill, in East Jylland, is probably Denmark's best-known mill, having appeared on a postage stamp. It was built in 1830 and restored in 1960, and has two overshot wheels, side-by-side. Another picturesque mill in Jylland is the half-timbered *Fulden Mill.* Fulden is comparatively modern (1908), and is turbine-driven. The mill with the largest waterwheel in Denmark (5.6 metres) is the Herregårds Mill at *Rødkilde,* which is thatched and half-timbered, dating from 1847.

King Christian IV had grand schemes for the old Gun Factory, Kronborg Geværfabrik, at *Hellebæk.* The Gun Factory was built in 1597, but before that Hellebæk already had a strip mill, smelting plant and copperfurnace. Local bog-iron was apparently used, with charcoal made from bog-alders. The Gun Factory was in production until 1870. At that time it had a barrel-grinding shop with two grindstones, each operated by its own over-shot waterwheel, two tilt-hammers worked by an undershot wheel and two bellows worked by another undershot wheel. In the drilling mill an overshot wheel drove a drilling frame and a bayonet grinding stone. Part of the factory has recently been restored.

The nearby *Eskrom Canal* was dug in 1802-5 to transport firewood from Grib Skov, but went out of commission in 1873, when the Grib Skov Railway was built. At the exit of the Canal a large waterwheel operated a grinding shop for the Gun Factory.

The activities on the Mølle river and at Hellebæk show the prime importance of waterpower to Danish industry as late as 1870, and also provide evidence of the great interest taken in these industries by the Crown.

Another notable example of industrial development initiated by the Crown is at *Frederiksværk.* In 1719 a canal was dug from Arresø to Roskilde Fjord, which provided plenty of water for industrial purposes at the Arresø end of the canal, and in 1728-29 the Crown set up an agate grinding mill on the south bank, a short distance from Arresø. A cannon factory was set up in 1751 and in 1756 the King granted the old agate and cannon works to Classen and Fabritius, on condition that they made gunpowder there. Classen became sole owner in 1767 and built a small harbour to facilitate transport to and from the works. In 1769 he added an iron-foundry and, later, a machine shop. The first steam engine to be built in Denmark, of 20 hp, came from Classen's shops at Frederiksværk in 1829. In 1820 there were 18 waterwheels at Frederiksværk, developing a total of 200 hp, and as late as the 1870s, Frederiksværk was described as 'the most significant industrial establishment in Denmark'. Several firms were then working parts of the works, one of which was Hærens Krudtværk, who ran the gunpowder mill. When they went out of commission in 1963, the works and machinery were preserved and now form the nucleus of the Black Gunpowder Museum which is being established under the control of the Army Museum (Tøjhusmuseet).

The windmill came into use in Denmark later than the water mill and usually only in places where the shortage of water made a watermill impossible to run. The best Danish windmills are in the Eastern part of the country, especially on the smaller islands. The finest is *Lundby Mill*, Falster, which is thatched to within about two metres of the ground and has been well restored.

TRANSPORT

The first railway to be built in Denmark ran from Copenhagen to Roskilde (1847). The best-preserved early railway, however, is from *Maribo* to *Bandholm*, which is the oldest private railway in Denmark (1869). It is now looked after by the Danish Railway Club, which operates it during the summer. The station at Bandholm is the original one.

One of the more remarkable railway stations in Denmark is the largely timber-built main station at *Copenhagen*, which dates from 1911. There are many nineteenth-century railway and road bridges which are of engineering interest, including the road bridge over the Gudenaa at *Randers*, built in 1823 and recently restored; the more recent steel bridge over the Little Belt (*Snognøy*), built in 1935; and the impressive Storstrøm Bridge (*Orehoved*) (1932–37).

The old dockyard and harbour equipment has nearly all disappeared, apart from warehouses. There are some attractive eighteenth-century warehouses at Nyhavn, not far from the centre of *Copenhagen*. In the Royal Dockyard one can still see the eighteenth-century crane (1784) (see plate 13), used for lifting ships' masts in and out. The crane proper is fixed to the top of the square brick tower, and its woodwork was renewed in 1922.

BREWING

The Danish determination to use the latest methods is not new. In the middle of the nineteenth century a new type of beer was developed in the Pilsen area of what is now Czechoslovakia. It was what brewers call a bottom-fermented beer, light in colour, with a slightly bitter taste of hops and sparkling with the chemist's addition of carbon-dioxide – very different from the traditional dark, top-fermented beer which Europeans had been drinking since the Middle Ages. The Tuborg Brewery in *Copenhagen* produced the new Pilsen-type beer from the time the brewery was first established, in 1873. At that time the old dark beer was being made at the King's Brew House in *Copenhagen*, now a sister company of Tuborg.

The Tuborg Brewery, one of the prominent features of Copenhagen's water-front, dates almost entirely since 1945. The other great Copenhagen brewing firm, Carlsberg, preserves much of the nineteenth-century atmosphere, partly by means of the brewery museum (Valby Langgade 1), which is as much a monument to the founders, Carl and Ottilia Jacobsen, as it is to brewing. The flavour of the Victorian virtues of charity, piety and patriotism is somewhat overwhelming. The gatehouse, supported by giant granite elephants, with its motto *Laboremus Pro Patria*, is a splendid symbol of a successful nineteenth-century family business.

AGRICULTURE

Commercial competition and increasingly strict public health regulations have long since made the nineteenth- and early twentieth-century milk and meat processing factories obsolete and indeed illegal, and little survives of their equipment outside museums. What is believed to have been Denmark's smallest milk-factory at *Mandø* (1897) was transferred in 1958 to the open-air museum at *Hjerl Hede* in Jutland. The factory is now equipped with old, but not original, machinery in working order, and is operated for a short period each summer. Another old milk-factory has, however, been preserved on its original site, at *Olgod* in West Jutland (see plate 69). Set up in 1882 it was Denmark's first commercial milk-processing factory, and was renovated and restored in 1950, using the original machinery.

Location of sites - Denmark*

Bandholm, north-east of Maribo	54.50N 11.30E	Map	9 EF 45
Børkop Mill, east of Velje	55.39N 9.39E	Map	9 DE 56
Copenhagen	55.43N 12.34E	Map	8 AB 12
Eskrom Canal	56.04N 12.34E	Map	8 AB 23

Frederiksværk	55.58N 12.02E	Map	7 FG 12
Fulden Mill, Jylland	56.05N 10.14E	Map	7 EF 12
Hellebæk, north-west of Helsingør	56.04N 12.34E	Map	8 AB 23
Hjerl Hede	56.42N 11.32E	Map	8 FG 12
Lundby Mill, north-west of Stubberkøping	54.48N 11.58E	Map	9 FG 45
Lyngby, near Holte	55.50N 12.29E	Map	8 AB 12
Mandø	55.17N 8.33E	Map	9 CD 45
Mølleaa, river north-west of Holte	55.48N 12.35E	Map	8 AB 12
Nysted, south-east of Maribo	54.40N 11.45E	Map	9 FG 45
Ølgod, south-east of Ringkøbing	55.44N 5.37E	Map	7 CD 12
Orehoved	54.58N 11.52E	Map	9 FG 45
Ørholm Mill	55.48N 12.35E	Map	8 AB 12
Randers, south-west of bridge carrying Gulleo-Velling road over river Gudenaa	56.23N 9.49E	Map	7 DE 12
Rødkilde, east of Fåborg	55.04N 10.24E	Map	9 DE 45
Snognøy	55.31N 9.43E	Map	9 DE 56
Strandmøllen	55.48N 12.35E	Map	8 AB 12

* *A.A. Continental Handbook, 1970–1*

FINLAND

The industrial development of Finland has been closely linked with its turbulent political history. Until 1809 it formed part of Sweden – Swedish is still a widely-used second language – and remained a very backward country, with few industries, apart from fishing and iron. From 1809 until 1817 Finland was an autonomous Russian Grand Duchy, becoming independent in 1917. The wars with the Soviet Union in 1939 and 1940 and between 1941 and 1944, and with Germany during 1944–45, caused great destruction and losses of territory, population and capital equipment. Remarkable efforts during the past 25 years, however, have made good the war-time setbacks and built a modern economy.

MUSEUMS

The Railway Museum (Rautatiemuseo) is at *Helsinki* Station. The first railway in Finland, from Helsinki to Hämeenlinna, was completed in 1862; the second line ran from Riihimäki to St Petersburg. Until 1917, the commercial link with Russia was of great importance to Finland, so it was natural to give priority to railways running in that direction, and the St Petersburg line provided a convenient and cheap method of getting paper and iron products to Russia. The Railway Museum has models of six of the earliest stations, all built in 1862. The wooden station at *Kerava* is the oldest surviving station, and is still in use (see plates 21, 22). The first locomotives to run in Finland were imported from England, but railway workshops were soon established at Helsinki and the first home-built engines came from there in 1874. The Railway Museum has several of the early locomotives, which are stored, together with coaches and

57

other large material, in the old engine sheds at Kaipiainen, Myllymäki, Hyvinkää and Karjaa. Also in *Helsinki* are the Post and Telegraph Museum (Tehtaankatn 21B), and the Bank Museum, at the Head Office of Ransallis-Osake Pankki (Aleksanterinkatu 42).

The importation and production of alcoholic drinks is a government monopoly in Finland. The government has a schnapps distillery at *Riihimäki*, and maintains a museum there, to illustrate the old days when distilling was carried out, legally, by peasants and larger landowners.

There is an open-air museum at *Fölisön* (Seurasaari) near Helsinki, which has windmills and fishermen's houses and equipment, and the Myllykoski Windmills Museum at *Uusikaupunki* (Nystad) should also be mentioned. There are many windmills still standing in the Åland Islands and the Ålands Museum at *Mariehamn* has interesting information about them. The Ålands Maritime Museum is also in Mariehamn; the Islands were much used as staging points by the Vikings, and the Museum documents the history of Finnish sailing ships from that time onwards. Its largest exhibit is the fourmasted sailing ship, 'Pommern', which is moored outside the Museum. Built in Glasgow in 1903, she achieved some fast times on the Australia run.

Finland has no national industrial or technical museum, but there is a local one at *Tampere* (Tampereen Kaupurgin Museolautakunta), originally private, but now run by the municipality in an old shoe factory. This contains, among other exhibits, a carding machine installed at Tampere by James Finlayson in 1824, which worked continuously until 1928, when it was replaced by a new machine. In 1820 Tsar Alexander I gave Finlayson the right to establish textile and engineering factories at Tampere. There is also a Handicrafts Museum at *Turku*.

IRON INDUSTRY

The Finnish iron industry was encouraged by Sweden during the seventeenth and eighteenth centuries, mainly because it provided an additional source of supply for munitions. The iron mines and iron bruks[1] are to be found within an area running north and west from Helsinki, towards Hangö in the west and Karkala in the north. The oldest iron mine is at *Ojamo*, near Lohja, which was in use from the fifteenth century until the middle of the eighteenth. Nowadays it presents the appearance of a water-filled pit in the middle of the woods, but its antiquity demands respect.

One of the earliest bruks still to survive as a commercial concern is *Svartå Bruk*. It was founded in 1561, and after a long career as an iron-working centre was converted to the manufacture of paper and cellulose.

[1] Industrial settlements. For a fuller explanation of this Swedish word, see below, p. 141.

A large modern plant is now concerned with its products. A number of workers' houses (1700) are still to be seen, together with the owner's house (1820) at *Vanjärvi*, close by. *Högfors Bruk* dates back to 1819, and the early furnace has been preserved. There has been extensive development during the present century, especially on the engineering side; new buildings were erected during the 1930s, and the works is now very large. It played an important part in the struggle against the Russians from 1941 until 1944, being one of Finland's principal sources of armaments. Another historic ironworks, although without the same recent growth as Högfors is at *Pojo*, on the opposite side of the lake from Svartå.

There is a well-preserved iron-making bruk at *Kauttua*, near Pori. It was founded in the late seventeenth century and was bought by its present owners, the Ahlström Company, in 1874. The eighteenth-century workers' houses, the administration building and the owner's house have been restored and preserved (see plates 44–46), as well as the main forge-building, which was erected in 1801. The same company owns *Strömfors Bruk* which has a museum and a tilt-hammer which was in use until comparatively recently (see plate 40), and a glassworks at *Karhula* which also has a museum.

Early material relating to the iron industry has also been preserved by another of Finland's large industrial concerns, Oy Fiskars. At *Billnäs Bruk* little remains of the eighteenth-century installations, apart from a blacksmith's cottage of about 1750. The company has, however, set up a museum at Billnäs, the collection being made up largely of examples of the axes, spades and other tools made at the forge. At *Skogby*, another site belonging to Oy Fiskars, there was at one time a small blast-furnace (1789) but it was blown down in 1904 and there are now only ruins to be seen.

TIMBER AND PAPER

The development of Finland's enormous timber resources came late. The first steam-driven sawmill began working in 1860 and the first pulp-mill in 1880. A sawmill of about 1900 is preserved at *Svartå Bruk* and there are others of the same vintage at *Trollböle*, near Ekenäs and *Grabbskog*.

When the new Institute building of the Finnish Pulp and Paper Research Institute in *Helsinki* was planned early in the 1860s, provision was made for a small paper museum. Many potential exhibits have already been lost, partly as a result of war, and partly because the rapid development of the Finnish pulp and paper industry during the present century caused material to disappear when mills and offices were modernised and rebuilt. Nevertheless, an excellent collection has already been accumulated to illustrate the history of papers and raw material, mainly in Finland.

There are many surviving monuments of the old, hand-made paper industry. The earliest is at *Tomasböle*, which dates from 1665. The village lies on the west side of the river, on the road from *Pojo* to *Tammisaari* (Ekenäs). The site of the mill is overgrown, but there are remains of the buildings and a memorial stone to indicate the importance of the site. The papermill buildings at *Möllby*, near Turku (Åbo) were put up in 1820 and are still intact, although since 1962 they have been used by a fish-canning company. *Tervakoski*, about 50 miles from Helsinki, which has been making paper since 1818, is still working and is the only place where one can see paper being made by the old process. The original mill no longer exists, and hand-made paper is produced in the new buildings on the occasions when there are orders for it. The greater part of the mill, however, is concerned entirely with machine-made paper.

TRANSPORT   Canals

Southern Finland is richly endowed with lakes and these, frozen and unfrozen, were the main means of inland transport before the coming of the railways. With such an elaborate natural system of rivers and lakes, together with a long coastline and hundreds of sea-inlets, little was needed in the way of man-made waterways. The *Saimaa Canal*, however (1856), is a significant transport monument. It was Finland's first canal and it made the transport of goods in the area a great deal easier. This canal connects Lake Saimaa, the largest lake chain in Europe, with the Gulf of Finland. It was completely rebuilt and widened after the 1945 war and was re-opened for passenger traffic in 1968. Another rebuilt canal can be seen at *Valkeakoski*. The old canal was completed in 1869 and the new one in 1953.

TOBACCO AND TAR

Two of Finland's old-established industries are identified with particular towns. The tobacco factories at *Pietarsaari* go back to the eighteenth century. One of them, Strengberg's, at Kaulukatu, just outside Pietarsaari, contains a museum devoted to the industry.

Oulu is an old market-town, where tar used to be brought down from the hinterland in long 'tar-boats' to be sold and exchanged for other commodities, and in the nineteenth century it was one of the world's most important ports for the tar trade. Unfortunately, the town was almost completely burnt down in 1822 and consequently nearly all the surviving buildings belong to the nineteenth and twentieth centuries, including some interesting warehouses in the inner harbour. Helsinki was similarly afflicted; in 1808 a great fire swept through the wooden buildings of the old town and destroyed practically everything.

Location of sites - **Finland***

Note: Many place-names in Finland are found in both their Swedish and Finnish forms, which often bear no resemblance whatever to one another. Some maps use one form, some another, and to avoid the resulting confusion where possible both forms have been given below.

Billnäs Bruk, north-east of Tammisaari (Ekenäs)	60.05N	23.37E	Map 3	EF 12
Fölisön (Seuressari), Helsinki	60.08N	25.00E	Map 3	EF 12
Grabbskog, north-west of Tammisaari (Ekenäs)	60.02N	23.23E	Map 3	EF 12
Högfors Bruk (Karkkila)	60.32N	24.11E	Map 3	EF 12
Karhula	60.29N	26.58E	Map 3	FG 12
Kauttua, (Kattua) south-east of Pori	61.29N	21.47E	Map 3	DE 23
Kerava, west of Borga	60.25N	25.10E	Map 3	EF 12
Mariehamn	60.05N	19.55E	Map 3	CD 12
Möllby, north-west of Turku (Åbo)	60.27N	22.17E	Map 3	DE 12
Ojamo, south-east of Lohja	60.14N	24.03E	Map 3	EF 12
Oulu	65.00N	25.26E	Map 3	DE 56
Pietarsaari (Jakobstad)	63.41N	22.40E	Map 3	DE 34
Pojo (Pohja), north-east of Tammisaari (Ekenäs)	60.06N	23.31E	Map 3	DE 12
Riihimäki	60.45N	24.45E	Map 3	EF 23
Saimaa Canal, connecting Lake Saimaa with the Gulf of Finland. Begins at	61.05N	28.18E	Map 3	FG 23
Skogby, east of Karkkila	60.21N	24.39E	Map 3	EF 12

Strömfors Bruk (Ruotsinpyhtad), south of Lovisa	60.32N 26.27E	Map	3	EF 12
Svartå Bruk, east of Lohja	60.08N 23.55E	Map	3	EF 12
Tammisaari (Ekenäs)	60.00N 23.32E	Map	3	DE 12
Tampere	61.32N 23.45E	Map	3	DE 23
Tervakoski, north-north-east of Helsinki	60.48N 24.37E	Map	3	EF 12
Tomasböle, north-west of Tammisaari (Ekenäs)	60.05N 23.32E	Map	3	DE 12
Trollböle, east of Ekenäs	60.00N 23.40E	Map	3	DE 12
Turku	60.27N 22.15E	Map	3	DE 12
Uusikaupunki (Nystad)	60.48N 20.30E	Map	3	DE 12
Valkeakoski	61.17N 24.05E	Map	3	DE 23

* *A.A. Continental Handbook, 1970–1*

FRANCE

The industrial development of France has shown, until very recently, two apparently contradictory features – an excellent system of higher technical training, organised and provided by the State, and an intense devotion to private ownership of the means of production. The family-controlled business continues to dominate French industry, despite its obvious weaknesses within a modern economy. There is, however, one important difference between family businesses in France and in the other countries of north-west Europe. The French industrial concern, with rare exceptions, has felt very little obligation to preserve the monuments of its past, in the way that is commonly found in, say, Germany or Sweden. It has, to this extent, a poorly developed sense of public responsibility. Company museums are therefore very few in France, and where they do exist they are all too likely to be little more than showrooms for today's products. There is little sentiment about French industry and, on the whole, little feeling for tradition and the past, except where – as in the case of wine and porcelain – tradition is exchangeable for cash. Since 1945 in particular there has been a great increase in the scale of mining and manufacturing and many of the old plants, where they existed, have been swept away. To go through parts of Lorraine or Strasbourg, or Bordeaux, for instance, is not unlike visiting the new industrial areas of Eastern Europe. Everything is large and up-to-date, and there is little evidence of the past, except in museums.

France gives its top engineers and managers considerable scope and pays them well. Civil engineering was considered as one of the professions very early in France: the Corps des Ingénieurs des Ponts et Chaussées was established in 1716 and by 1747 it had its own college, the Ecole des Ponts et Chaussées. The first director of the college was the great bridge-designer,

Jean Perronet, whose work included the Neuilly Bridge, replaced in 1956, over the Seine (the design, with its bevelled arches, was copied in England by Telford in his bridge at Over, near Gloucester, which still stands), the Pont Ste Maxence over the Oise, and the Pont de la Concorde (1791) in *Paris*. The Ecole Polytechnique, the great French establishment for training the higher levels of professional engineers, was a creation of the Revolution, founded by the National Convention in 1792.

MUSEUMS

There are two national museums in *Paris*, which cover the field of industrial and technical history. One forms part of the Conservatoire National des Arts et Métiers at 292 rue St Martin, set up under the Convention in 1794. There is nothing exactly like the Conservatoire outside the Communist countries. It organises evening courses in science and technology, operates testing and control laboratories, and runs a museum (opened in 1802), where the progress of technology is illustrated with models, originals of machines, drawings and photographs. The Musée des Arts et Traditions Populaires (Palais de Chaillot, Place du Trocadéro) has a large section devoted to early manufacturing techniques, the Département de l'Artisanat. This aims to systematise the study of pre-industrial crafts before they finally disappear and to collect both tools and the products at different stages of manufacture.

The French have a highly integrated system of museums, which has no real parallel elsewhere. The Director of the Musée du Louvre also carries the title of Director of Museums in France and is a person of considerable power in the world of preservation. Partly because the organisation of museums is such a professional affair, there is a strong tendency to believe that what cannot be transferred to a museum is hardly worth preserving, although industrial monuments with strongly marked architectural merits are sometimes brought under the care of the Ministry of Fine Arts.

SALTWORKS

A good example of an industrial relic which has been considered worthy of this treatment is the saltworks at *Arc-et-Senans* (see plates 36, 37 and 38), 32 kilometres south of Besançon. It is usually called the Saline de Chaux after the nearby Forest of Chaux. It was a grand concept, built in the 1770s by Claude-Nicolas Ledoux, at that time Inspector of the Royal Saltworks. Salt was then a royal monopoly, and heavily taxed. A salt spring was discovered near the Swiss border and the brine was taken ten miles by pipeline to the new works, so that the forest-wood could be used in the evaporating-furnaces. The brine contained only 11 grammes of salt per litre, compared with 38 grammes at the saltworks on the Mediterranean coast, so the works were never economic and they were closed down on several occasions, the last being in 1920. The Company, appalled by the prospect of having a national monument on their hands, then dynamited several of the buildings. What remains has since been carefully repaired at the expense of the State.

Ledoux planned an ideal city based on the saltworks – an enormous oval, with the saltworks in the centre – but the Revolution put an end to building. By then, there was a grand entrance, a semi-circle of warehouses, guardrooms and similar buildings, with a splendid director's house (really the administration building) and a row of factory buildings.

Salt is still produced by the open-pan method on the Mediterranean coast between Sète and *Agde*, where the great white heaps of dried salt are an interesting feature of the landscape. Inland, the great salt deposits of Lorraine have been exploited since Roman times. A number of local place-names contain a salt-element; Château-Salins, Rosières-aux-Salines, and so on. The modern salt-industry in Lorraine is very large and highly industrialised.

WINDMILLS

On the *Ile Noirmoutier* on the Atlantic coast, salt-making is assisted by a curious system of midget windmills. Noirmoutier once had dozens of windmills of the normal type, and those which are left show that they were built on the pattern of the Vendée tower-mills. Such traditional mills can still be seen at *La Fosse* and *Barbâtre*, most of them grouped between Herbaudière and Barbâtre, but none of them are now in use. The salt-makers' mills are still working, but they are so small that they are hardly noticeable from a distance. Their purpose is to speed up the salt gathering so that the new season's salt can be sold at the same time as that from the Mediterranean. They pump up the water which has deposited the salt in the last pans of the salt marshes and discharge it into one of the numerous canals, and as the lift never exceeds one metre, the tiny windmills are perfectly adequate. The sails are made of sheet iron. The mills are taken to pieces and stored after the end of the salt-making season, which lasts from May to September.

Probably the best-known windmill in France is the two-storeyed tower-mill at *Fontvielle*, which was built in 1814 and is preserved as a memorial to Alphonse Daudet. Fontvielle, in the Département of Bouches-du-Rhône in Provence, had four tower-mills, of which the Moulin St-Pierre was both the most recent and the last to close down, in 1915. A period of decay followed, until the Société des Amis des Moulins d'Alphonse Daudet was set up in 1933, and acquired and restored the mill, opening it to the public in 1935. The adjacent bolting-house was converted into a museum at the same time. The Moulin St-Pierre was chosen for restoration as it was the most complete of the four. It represents well Maître Cornille's mill in *Lettres de Mon Moulin*. The other three mills are preserved as masonry-shells.

Another famous windmill which has been preserved is at *Valmy*, a village in the Marne where the Prussians were defeated in 1792, a battle celebrated by Goethe.

TRANSPORT   Bridges and Aqueducts

The earliest industrial monument in France, the *Pont-du-Gard*, near *Nîmes* (see plate 2) is also under the most careful State protection. It was built in 18 BC, on the orders of Agrippa, and its three tiers of arches carry a water-supply over the River Gard. The Pont-du-Gard is one of the great civil engineering wonders of the world. The stones which form its arches were so perfectly cut that they needed no mortar to keep them in place.

Hardly in the same class as the Pont-du-Gard, but impressive even so, is the 1843 *Zola Dam* across the valley of the Infernet, in Provence. It provides the water supply for Aix-en-Provence.

Among the more modern French viaducts of distinction are the *Garabit viaduct* over the Truyère river, built to the design of Gustave Eiffel in 1885, which has a central span of 164 metres, and the *Viaur viaduct* (1898) at Aveyron, with an arch of 219 metres, which was the first big bridge in France to be constructed of steel. One of the earliest concrete bridges in the world is Hennebique's famous *Pont de Châtellerault*, which dates from 1898.

TRANSPORT   Canals

France was a pioneer in the construction of canals. The locked *Briare Canal* connecting the Loire with the Seine, was completed in 1642, and the *Burgundy Canal* was cut in the first half of the seventeenth century. It runs from the River Yonne to the Saône and has 189 locks. The great achievement of that century was, however, the Languedoc Canal – the Canal du Midi, connecting the Atlantic and the Mediterranean by way of the Garonne. Designed by Riquet, it took fifteen years to build and was opened to traffic in 1681. 290 kilometres long, 80.4 metres wide and 1.8 metres deep, it begins at *Toulouse* and ends near Agde, at the *Etang de Thau*. It crosses the Col de Naraize by means of 65 locks and a tunnel.

In the late nineteenth century it was bought by the Midi Railway, in order to divert traffic to the railway. It then fell into a bad state of repair and was bought by the Government in 1898. Despite considerable subsequent expenditure it is still only 1.8 metres deep and is not really commercially viable.

TRANSPORT Railways

Transport has not yet been made to fit conveniently into the official French pattern of museums. There is no national museum of transport or railways. The gap is filled to some extent by the Malakoff Museum of AMTUIR (Association pour le Musée des Transports Urbains, Interurbains et Ruraux), which is housed in an old tramway depot at *Malakoff*, a suburb of Paris, and is open on the first Sunday in each month.

A few of the grand style railway stations have survived the inexorable process of modernisation. In *Paris* the Gare d'Orsay is closed, but the magnificent Gare de Lyon (1895) survives, together with its wonderful pre-1914 restaurant. The Gare du Nord (1864) (see plate 17), the Gare St-Lazare (1885) (see plate 18) and the Gare de L'Est (1874) have not been greatly changed. One of the finest pieces of railway architecture anywhere in Europe is the Bénédictin station at *Limoges*, a noble palace of white stone, with a clock tower and central dome, dating from 1929. The park and lake in front allow the station to be seen to perfection. Another fine station is *Metz*, built in 1902.

The first major railway in France, Paris-Rouen, and then on to Le Havre, was built by a British engineer, Joseph Locke, and the great British contractor, Thomas Brassey, using mainly British workmen. The 93.3-kilometre Rouen-Le Havre section, completed in 1843, was characterised by almost continuous tunnels, viaducts and embankments and the most formidable gradients encountered by railway builders. Perhaps its greatest monument is the *Barentin viaduct*, 19.3 kilometres from Rouen. It has 27 brick-built arches, 30 metres high, each with a span of 15 metres. Following torrential rain, the viaduct collapsed a few weeks after it was opened, but was rebuilt by Brassey in six months at his own expense. Among the other French railways built by Brassey were Orléans-Bordeaux (1842–50), Paris-Cherbourg (1852–55) and Lyon-Avignon (1852).

TRANSPORT Docks

The railway to Cherbourg was built to increase the effectiveness of the port as a naval base. The docks and arsenal at *Cherbourg* had been begun by Louis XIV and were completed by Louis Napoleon. An important part of the scheme was the great breakwater, the Digue Centrale, designed by de Cessant. An ingenious method of construction was used: 21 towers, in the form of truncated cones, were built by shipwrights, using oak and beech as materials. These towers were then floated into position and sunk along the line of of the future breakwater, and were filled and covered with stone. The cones were gradually eaten away by boring-insects and disappeared within four years, but the stones fell into their natural slope and provided the core of a permanent breakwater. The breakwater, which is 4.8 kilometres long, was begun just after the Revolution, but not completed until 1853.

One of the odder coastal monuments in France is the *Cordouan lighthouse* on the Gironde estuary, near Royan. This sixteenth-century building is on a small island and its fine rooms were originally designed entirely for domestic use, the lantern being added as an afterthought during the reign of Louis XV. The architect of Cordouan was Louis de Foix, who also designed the Escurial Palace near Madrid.

WINE INDUSTRY

The variety of French industries is very wide, as one would expect in a country with such a range of climate and natural resources. One finds, for instance, coal in the north and east, tobacco factories and tobacco growing in the south-west, glassworks in the Vosges, breweries around Nancy, textiles along the valleys west of Rouen, porcelain at Sèvres and Limoges. All have some monuments of their past. Yet one has to select and it is natural, perhaps, to give special consideration to the wine industry, partly because of its long history and economic importance and partly because vineyards characterise such a considerable part of the French landscape. Many of the vineyards are of great antiquity and are themselves the most important monuments of the industry – French tourist literature suggests routes to see them, the Wine Roads – but one can instance other monuments which cover rather less ground. At both *Epernay* and *Rheims* there are cellars cut in the chalk where wine ages gracefully and these cellars are accessible to the public. What might possibly be taken for old wine cellars at *Meschers*, near Talmont, Charente-Maritime, are in fact former stone-quarries, now skilfully and profitably converted into restaurants. *Epernay* also has an excellent museum in the Château Perrier devoted to the history of the champagne vineyards and of wine-making, the Musée du Vin de Champagne; while the Champagne Mercier Museum includes a collection of early wine presses (Musée de Pressoirs). Poitou, Land of Cognac, has, however, no public museum similarly devoted to cognac.

11 Shipbuilding Dock, Motala, Sweden. 1822. The oldest in Sweden. Built, together with the adjoining workshops, by Baltzar von Platen, who was responsible for the Göta Canal. (*see page* 145)

12 Harbour Crane, Hamburg, West Germany. 1858. Built to replace a famous wooden crane, of very similar design, which fell to pieces the previous year. (*see page* 166)

13 Crane, Royal Dockyard, Copenhagen, Denmark. 1784. Used mainly for stepping and unstepping the masts of warships. Restored in 1922. (*see page* 53)

14 Merchants' Houses, Hanseatic Quarter, Bergen, Norway. Fifteenth century. These wooden houses have miraculously escaped the numerous fires which destroyed so many buildings in the Scandinavian towns. (*see page* 110)

15 Detail of Merchant's House, Bergen. The Hanseatic merchants trading from Bergen were a prosperous community and their houses and warehouses reflected their wealth.

16 Warehouses, Trondheim, Norway. Seventeenth century. A simple, straight-forward style of construction, in contrast to the more elaborate buildings of the more prosperous Bergen.

17 Gare du Nord, Paris, France. 1864. A splendid example of the grand style which was felt appropriate to important public buildings at a time when the central parts of Paris were being replanned and rebuilt. (*see page* 67)

18 Gare St-Lazare, Paris, France. 1889. The fine train-shed, shown in this photograph, has suffered very few changes since it was erected. (*see page* 67)

19 Temple Meads Station, Bristol, England. 1838–40. The original terminus of Brunel's Great Western line from Paddington to Bristol. Now used as a covered car-park.

20 Helen's Bay Railway Station, Northern Ireland. 1863–64. The arms of the Marquis of Dufferin and Ava can be seen on the gable end. (*see page 32*)

21 Railway Station, Kerava, Finland. 1867. Photograph taken in 1908. The oldest surviving station in Finland. (*see page* 57)

22 Railway Station, Kerava, in 1969, showing new track-bed under construction as part of an electrification project.

23 Railway Station, Drevja, Norway. 1864. Norway's oldest station. On the Nordland railways constructed through very difficult country.

24 Rossio Railway Station, Lisbon, Portugal. 1875. One of the oldest surviving railway termini in Portugal. (*see page* 122)

25 Central Station, Milan, Italy. 1924–31. One of the largest railway stations in Europe. (*see page* 95)

26 Windmills, Mykonos, Greece. Repeatedly restored as a tourist attraction. The originals may date from the seventeenth century. (*see page* 85)

27 Windmills, Kinderdijk, Netherlands. 1738–60. The most impressive mill landscapes in the Netherlands, with 19 mills working in an integrated drainage scheme. (*see page* 103)

28 Grander Mühle, Trittau, West Germany. *c.* 1750. This watermill was on an estate formerly belonging to Bismarck; it has been restored and is preserved as a national monument.

29 Sawmill, Saltvik: interior, showing 4-gang saw. This technique, established as early as the eighteenth century, allowed a high annual output of sawn timber with a minimum number of men, an important factor in a country where labour was scarce.

30 Waterdriven sawmill, Saltvik, Åland, Finland. 1909. Power-driven sawmills were in use in Sweden and Finland as early as the seventeenth century.

31 Combined sawmill and cornmill, Mattas i Krogstad, Åland, Finland. 1934.
This very practical mill uses the sawmill as a pedestal for the windmill, thus
exposing its mill-sweeps more effectively to the wind.

32 Water-powered fulling mill, Cookstown, Northern Ireland. *c.* 1760. Now being restored by the Northern Ireland Committee of the National Trust. Mills of this type were formerly very numerous in the textile areas of Ulster. Most of them have now either disappeared or are in a ruinous condition.

33 Waldemarsudde oil-seed mill, Stockholm, Sweden. 1784. The complex system of massive wooden machinery is in excellent condition. The mill has been twice restored, in 1900 and 1960. (*see page* 145)

34 The Great Mill, Gdansk, Poland. Mid-fourteenth century, subsequently restored. The Mill is the gabled, seven-storeyed building to the right of the picture. The tall building, with its roof projecting over the ship's flag, is the seventeenth-century dockyard crane, also recently restored. (*see page* 118)

TOBACCO

Bergerac, an important centre for tobacco-growing in France, has a Musée du Tabac in the town hall, with exhibits showing the history of the tobacco industry and tobacco trade.

PAPER AND TEXTILES

The mid-eighteenth century hand-made paper mill of Richard de Bas, at *Ambert*, Puy-de-Dôme (see plates 56, 57), has been preserved as a working museum, the Musée Historique du Papier. It contains a remarkable set of water-driven wooden beaters for preparing the rags.

At *Troyes*, in the town's historical museum, the Musée Historique de Troyes, Hôtel Vauluisant, there is a special section for the hosiery and knitted trades (Musée de la Bonneterie). Troyes is the centre of this industry in France; stocking-frames were set up there in 1745, in the Hôpital de la Trinité, in order to give the orphans accommodated there a chance to earn a living. The Musée de la Bonneterie has, among the numerous eighteenth- and nineteenth-century machines in its fine collection, one of the first stocking-frames to be used at the Hôpital de la Trinité.

IRON AND COAL

The Meuse valley from Sedan to Givet in the Ardennes had an iron industry from the Middle Ages onwards, using the abundant local supplies of charcoal and water-power from the tributaries of the Meuse. Place names such as Neuve-Forge and Vieille-Forge commemorate the old industry. Nowadays, however, the French iron industry is almost synonymous with Lorraine.

The iron deposits of Lorraine rank with those of Kursk in Siberia and Lake Superior in America as the richest in the world, and make France the third largest producer of iron-ore. The Lorraine deposits were not worked, however, until 1878, when the discovery of the Thomas process made it possible to free the ore of the phosphorous content which had hitherto made it unusable. Much the same is true of the Lorraine coalfields, where the surface equipment is extremely modern. At *Saint-Etienne*, Loire, however, in the oldest coal-mining area in France, there is an excellent mining museum, the Musée de la Mine, which contains two full-sized sections of mine-gallery, one of the old type and the other modern. The iron industry has its museum at *Nancy*, the large and well-arranged Musée de l'Histoire de Fer, opened in 1966. The museum is in a new building, designed for the purpose, and was conceived from the start as a museum of the history of iron and not simply of the iron and steel industry.

CONCRETE AND IRON-FRAMED BUILDINGS

French engineers and architects have made a notable contribution to the development of building technology. The reinforced concrete bridge at Châtellerault, by François Hennebique, has already been mentioned. It was preceded in 1895 by the same architect's spinning-mill at *Tourcoing*, one of the first buildings in the world to use structural reinforced concrete. Two other pioneering constructions in reinforced concrete are the airship hangar at *Orly*, designed by Freysinnet and completed in 1916, and Auguste Perret's famous garage in the Rue de Ponthieu (1905), *Paris* (see plate 63), which has unfortunately been allowed to become dilapidated and may be demolished. Another industrial building to hold an honoured place in the history of architecture is the Menier chocolate factory at *Noisiel-sur-Maine*. It was finished in 1872, the architect being Jules Saulnier, and was the first building of any size to use an iron frame throughout.

Location of sites - **France***

Agde	43.37N	1.26E	Map 22	AB 45
Ambert	45.33N	3.45E	Map 17	AB 34
Arc-et-Senans, south-west of Besançon	47.02N	5.46E	Map 13	FG 12
Barentin viaduct	49.33N	0.57E	Map 13	AB 56
Bergerac	44.50N	0.29E	Map 16	CD 23
Briare Canal	47.38N	2.44E	Map 13	CD 23
Burgundy Canal, at Attigny, north-west of Vouziers	49.28N	4.35E	Map 13	EF 45
Châtellerault	46.49N	0.33E	Map 12	FG 12
Cherbourg	49.38N	1.37W	Map 12	DE 56
Cordouan	45.36N	1.10W	Map 16	AB 45
Epernay	49.02N	3.58E	Map 13	DE 45
Etang de Thau, near Agde	43.19N	3.29E	Map 21	EF 56

Fontvielle, south-west   43.43N   4.42E   Map 22 CD 56
of Tarascon

Garabit viaduct, south-   44.90N   3.08E   Map 16 FG 23
west of St Flour

La Fosse and Barbâtre,   47.00N   2.15W   Map 12 CD 12
Ile Noirmoutier
Limoges   45.50N   1.15E   Map 16 DE 45

Meschers, west of Cozes   45.34N   0.57W   Map 16 AB 45
Metz   49.08N   6.10E   Map 14 AB 45

Nancy   48.42N   6.12E   Map 14 AB 34
Nîmes   43.50N   4.21E   Map 22 BC 56
Noisiel-sur-Maine,   48.51N   2.38E   Map 13 CD 45
south-west of Lagny

Orly   48.45N   2.24E   Map 13 CD 34

Paris   48.52N   2.20E   Map 13 CD 45
Pont de Châtellerault   46.49N   0.33E   Map 12 FG 12
Pont-du-Gard, near   43.57N   4.32E   Map 22 CD 56
Nîmes

Rheims   49.15N   4.02E   Map 13 DE 45

Saint-Etienne   45.26N   4.23E   Map 17 BC 34

Toulouse   43.33N   1.24E   Map 21 BC 56
Tourcoing   50.43N   3.09E   Map 10 DE 12
Troyes   48.18N   4.05E   Map 13 DE 34

Valmy, south-west of   49.05N   4.46E   Map 13 EF 45
Verdun
Viaur viaduct, north of   44.07N   2.18E   Map 16 EF 12
Tanus

Zola Dam, south-east   43.28N   5.27E   Map 22 DE 45
of Aix-en-Provence

* *A.A. Continental Handbook, 1970–1*

GERMAN DEMOCRATIC REPUBLIC

In the German Democratic Republic industrial monuments are greatly esteemed and well looked after, on the grounds that they contribute to a proper understanding of history. Castles, churches, palaces, it is felt, are the symbols of the old imperialist, capitalist élite, as half-timbered farm-houses and villages embodied the Blood and Earth philosophy of the Nazis. These essentially capitalist, reactionary objects were the monuments which received most care, attention and money until the outbreak of war in 1939. Since the establishment of a socialist system, however, the position has changed; the task now is seen to be to popularise the history of the means of production, and for this it is essential to preserve technical monuments and to present them in a meaningful way. They represent and help to explain a progressive, democratic view of history.

Until 1952, however, practice lagged sadly behind theory, since to qualify for preservation as an historic monument a building had to have been created before 1850. This ruled out, for instance, the monuments of the brown-coal industry, which only developed to a significant extent after 1860, but which is of great importance for any historical study of the German economy. In 1952 the GDR brought in its first legislation for the preservation of historic monuments. It defined a technical monument as something which was either:

(a) a landmark in the development of the means of production, or
(b) representative of a clearly marked technical period of development, or
(c) typical of the production methods in use within a particular region.

With this legal support, a thoroughgoing national inventory of industrial monuments was undertaken. Material was classified as belonging to one of five categories:

(1) Mining.
(2) Smelting, metal-working and machine-building.
(3) Textiles and light industry.
(4) Building materials and chemicals.
(5) Small workshops, arts and crafts.

The ideal, however, has not yet been realised, and in East Germany as elsewhere, precious material has been lost because action could not be taken sufficiently quickly. The oldest surviving briquette press (1873), an important item in the brown-coal industry, was destroyed in 1968, and a 3,000 hp Sulzer steam-engine (1903), regarded as one of the finest steam-engines ever built, was scrapped before it could be officially labelled a technical monument.

Even so, a very great deal has been achieved, and it is probably safe to say that the preservation of industrial monuments is being carried out more methodically and effectively in East Germany than in any other country, with the possible exception of Poland.

MUSEUMS

Museums in the GDR are considered to be integral parts of the educational process. The Museum for German History (Museum für Deutsche Geschichte, 108 Unter den Linden 2) in *Berlin* presents in a brilliantly professional way the whole panorama of German thought and achievement since 1789. The history of industry and technology is presented as an essential element in the development of the nation. A similar emphasis is noticeable in the Mining Museum (Stadt- und Bergbaumuseum, Akademiestrasse 6) in *Freiberg*, and in most of the local museums, for example, the Städtisches Heimatmuseum in Schloss Branitz in *Cottbus*, the Landesmuseum in the Museumplatz in *Weimar* and the Städtisches Museum in *Zwickau*.

The Museum of Transport in *Dresden* (Augustus Strasse 1) has a very good collection of what one might call portable transport items – old coaches, locomotives, signal equipment and so on. Most of the non-portable material – bridges, stations, tunnels – is still in use and requires little protection, apart from normal maintenance and watchfulness against insensitive and unnecessary alteration and rebuilding. In *Magdeburg* the Museum of Cultural History at Otto von Guerickstrasse 68 has a section devoted to technology and in *Jena*, in the Planetarium, there is the Carl-Zeiss Museum of Optics.

There is, as yet, no open-air museum in the GDR as such, but a number of the industrial complexes are, in fact, giant open-air museums, devoted to industry.

COALMINING

For hard-coal mining, there are several representative sites, one of the most important being in the *Oelsnitz-Erzgebirge* area, near Karl-Marx-Stadt. A group of old-established pits has been selected to illustrate the development of mining techniques within the past 150 years. These include the surface installations at the Gottessegen pit (1860), the Hedwig pit (1885), the Albert Funk pits (1920) and the Karl Liebknecht pit (1922–5). The Oelsnitz area has had a worldwide reputation for its pioneering work in the field of pit-head winding gear. The plan here is to make the Karl Liebknecht pit the museum centre and at the other pits to preserve only the pit-head gear. A second 'central monument' (zentrales technisches Denkmal) for the hard-coal industry is the Hoffnungs pit at *Zwickau*, which was one of the first big pits in Germany (1844) and the first to operate its haulage gear by electricity. The pit ceased working in 1966.

A similar plan has been adopted for the brown-coal industry. Here the centre is *Zeitz*, near Halle. The monument-complex (Denkmalcomplex) consists of three elements – the Paul II pit, the Zeitz briquette plant (1880) and the tar-distillery at Groitzchen. As they stand at present, these all illustrate the early days of the brown-coal industry, but by bringing in later plant from elsewhere it will be possible to present a complete picture of the technical growth of the industry over a period of something like seventy years.

POTASH AND TIN

Two centres of the potash industry have been considered suitable for preservation. At the Berlepsch-Maybach pits at *Stassfurt*, near Magdeburg, there are two shafts and it may eventually be possible to allow tourists to visit the enormous underground caverns, which are as much as 80 metres high in places, from which the potash has been extracted. Stassfurt is of international importance, because potassium salts were first discovered here and the first pits in the world were sunk to extract them. The second site is the Glückauf potash works at *Sondershausen*, near Erfurt. The pit-head gear at the Glückauf 2 pit, next to the railway station at Sonderhausen, is a remarkable achievement in steel-construction, but the underground workings are not as spectacular here as at Stassfurt.

The plant for washing tin-ore at *Altenberg*, near Dresden, has been preserved as an example of the tin-working techniques which were in use in the area during the sixteenth to nineteenth centuries.

SALTWORKS

The technical history of the salt industry can be studied at four places. At *Halle* there is a boiling house, with the pans still in working condition, workers' houses dating from the early nineteenth century, and the Hallorenmuseum. At *Bad Sulza*, near Erfurt, there is still much to be seen, despite the transfer of some of the equipment to Halle. There are two towers, where borings were made to reach the brine; both old and new methods of bringing the brine to the surface – the old methods include the only completely preserved hand-operated gin in the GDR – and five boiling-houses, whose chimneys are an impressive feature of the landscape. Four of the five boiling-houses now receive brine from the VEB works at Weimar, not from Sulza. The fifth is no longer operational and is being converted into a museum.

At *Kösen*, near Halle, there is an arrangement (1730) for raising brine which is of great technological importance (see plate 35). It consists of a waterwheel driving rods which connect, under a belfry-like structure, with a double-rod system for bringing brine up the shaft, and is the only system of its kind to have been preserved intact. Other interesting remains of the old salt industry are to be found at *Witzleben*, in the Dürrenberg area, which has shafts dating from the eighteenth and early nineteenth centuries, and *Bad Salzelmer*, near Magdeburg.

IRON INDUSTRY

The most important early iron-ore and coal mines are in the *Freiberg* area. The installations here are being restored and preserved to show the development of mining techniques from the sixteenth to the twentieth centuries. Individual items include the surface-equipment at the Abraham pit (see plate 52), including the 1839 pumping tower and pit-head gear; the 1848 pit-head gear at the Alte Elisabeth pit; the 1856 waterwheel, working 80 metres below the surface at the Rote Grube pit, and the stone-built drainage canal exit at Muldental.

The Happelshütte ironworks (1835) at *Schmalkalden* has one of the very few surviving charcoal blast-furnaces in Central Europe. Studied together with the demonstration iron-ore mine at Arbach and the Wilhelmsburg Museum in Schmalkalden, it provides an opportunity of understanding the development of iron-production from the eighteenth century up to the present day. Happelshütte is to be compared with *Wocklum* in the Ruhr, details of which are given in the section on West Germany. The buildings have been recently restored and include a large charcoal-store of considerable architectural interest.

The ironworks at *Peitz*, near Cottbus, has been rebuilt several times since production began on the site in the early sixteenth century. The present premises date from 1812. Peitz ceased to operate as an ironworks in the 1860s, when parts of the buildings were used as a textile factory. The buildings, which have been restored, are architecturally very pleasing.

An exceptionally interesting iron-foundry is at *Mägdesprung*, near Harzgerode. In the first part of the nineteenth century Mägdesprung centred its activities on a blast-furnace. The owner's house, in which a fine collection of decorative ironwork can be seen, survives from this period, together with a number of workers' cottages and other smaller buildings. Later, the works was converted into a foundry and a good deal of the early equipment is still there, including the cupola furnaces.

The Frohnauer forge (1616) near *Annaberg*, in the Halle district, has three water-driven hammers. It was damaged during the Second World War and restored in 1953. At *Freibergsdorf*, near Freiberg, there is a water-driven hammer still in operation. The metal worked here is copper.

LIME

The mid-nineteenth century limekilns at *Rüdersdorf*, near Berlin, and *Lengefeld*, in the Erzgebirge, have been preserved, and at the latter site one can see the whole process in operation, from the quarry to the final product. Lengefeld has a special claim to the visitor's attention, since it was here that the paintings from the Staatliche Kunstsammlungen in Dresden were hidden for safety in 1945. Lime has been produced at Lengefeld since the sixteenth century, the oldest kiln still operating was built in 1836. Another nineteenth-century kiln, at *Wriezen*, in the Bad Freienwalde district, only stopped working in 1926.

TRANSPORT

The transport monuments preserved on-site include the wooden covered bridges at *Metzdorf* in Saxony and at *Wünschendorf*, near Gera. A well-known early railway viaduct is at *Göltzchtal* (see plate 3), between Reichenbach and Plauen. It was built between 1845 and 1851, on the pattern of the Roman viaducts, with three rows of arches, varying between 14 and 17 metres in width, and is 579 metres long. The oldest surviving railway terminus in the GDR is the Bayrischer Bahnhof in *Leipzig* (1845).

The GDR has only a short coastline, but it contains one or two old lighthouses of some historic interest, chief among them the *Cape Arkona* lighthouse on the island of Rügen.

WINDMILLS AND WATERMILLS

The preservation of windmills and watermills tends to be regarded in the GDR as something of a romantic aberration, unconnected with the serious business of industrial and technical history. A few mills unconnected with industrial plants have, however, been preserved as examples of a long-dead technology. They include windmills at *Naumburg, Saritsch* and *Eckartsberga*, a boat-mill at *Düben*, on the River Mulde, and a pumping mill on the Spree at *Cottbus*. The fine post-mill at Saritsch, in the Bautzen district, was severely damaged during the 1939–45 war, but restored and made operable again in 1954.

The oil-mill at *Neuhausen*, in the Marienberj district of the Erzgebirge, is 300 years old; it has six pairs of stamps.

Location of sites - German Democratic Republic*

Annaberg	50.35N 13.01E	Map 4	CB 56
Altenburg, west of Dresden	50.46N 13.46E	Map 2	DE 56
Bad Salzelmer, south of Magdeburg	52.00N 11.48E	Map 2	CD 23
Bad Sulza, south-west of Naumburg	51.05N 11.37E	Map 2	CD 12
Cape Arkona lighthouse, island of Rügen	54.65N 12.28E	Map 2	DE 56
Cottbus	51.43N 14.21E	Map 2	EF 23
Düben, north-west of Falckenburg	51.36N 12.35E	Map 2	DE 12
Eckartsberga, north-west of Weimar	51.07N 11.34.	Map 2	BC 12
Freiberg	50.55N 13.21E	Map 4	DE 56
Freibergsdorf	50.55N 13.21E	Map 4	DE 56

Göltzchtal, between Reichenbach and Plauen	50.37N 12.18E and 50.30N 12.08E	Map	4	CD 56
		Map	4	CD 56
Halle	51.28N 11.58E	Map	2	CD 12
Kösen, near Halle	51.26N 11.56E	Map	2	CD 12
Lengefeld, south-east of Reichenbach	50.44N 13.12E	Map	4	DE 56
Leipzig	51.20N 12.20E	Map	2	CD 12
Mägdesprung, south of Magdeburg	51.41N 11.09E	Map	2	CD 23
Marienberg	50.41N 13.29E	Map	4	DE 56
Metzdorf, south-south-west of Wrietzen	52.35N 14.05E	Map	2	DE 34
Naumburg	51.09N 11.48E	Map	2	CD 12
Neuhausen, near Marienberg	50.41N 13.29E	Map	4	DE 56
Oelsnitz-Erzegeberge area, west of Karl-Marx-Stadt	50.50N 12.55E	Map	4	CD 56
Peitz, north-east of Cottbus	51.43N 14.21E	Map	2	EF 23
Rüdersdorf, east of Berlin	52.29N 13.47E	Map	2	DE 23
Saritsch, north-east of Bautzen	51.15N 14.30E	Map	2	EF 12
Schmalkalden	50.43N 10.28E	Map	4	AB 56
Sondershausen, east of Leipzig	51.23N 10.52E	Map	2	CD 12
Stassfurt	51.51N 11.35E	Map	2	CD 23
Witzleben	51.18N 12.04E	Map	2	CD 12
Wriezen	52.43N 14.09E	Map	2	DE 34
Wünschendorf, north-east of Gera	50.51N 12.11E	Map	4	CD 56
Zeitz	51.03N 12.08E	Map	2	CD 12
Zwickau	50.43N 12.30E	Map	4	CD 56

* *A.A. Continental Handbook, 1970–1*

GREECE

During the long period of Turkish rule, which lasted from 1453 until 1827, Greece was an almost purely agricultural country. The first industrial revolution passed her by and she is, even now, the most backward country in Europe, East or West. As a member of the twentieth-century technological world, she has few natural resources, but her tourist capital is, of course, immense and the money brought in by foreign tourists represents a very important part of her national income.

80 per cent. of Greece is mountainous, 85 per cent. of all agricultural units are of less than five hectares, and there is no oil, very little iron-ore, no heavy industry, no hard coal, although lignite is mined at Aliveri, in Euboea, and Ptolemais, in Macedonia. As some compensation for this, there are considerable deposits of bauxite at Distomon, on Parnassus and of several of the more valuable metallic ores.

Domestic industry has been widespread in Greece for several centuries. During the seventeenth and eighteenth centuries, *Zagora*, for example, 47 kilometres east of Volas, was an important commercial centre, with a well-developed export trade in locally-manufactured woollen products. The stately merchant's houses and warehouses of this period are evidence of the town's former prosperity. The island of Mykonos is still famous for its hand-woven fabrics. But Greek industry, in the strict sense of the word, is post-1945 and great efforts have been made in recent years to improve the country's industrial potential. The rivers are mostly narrow, shallow and unfit for navigation, but tend to be fast-flowing and hydro-electric plants have been constructed on a number of them – on the Ladon in the Peloponnese, on the Louron in Epirus, and on the Agras and the Edessa in Macedonia. An oil refinery has been built in the Bay of Eleusis, and the Niarchos shipyard at Salamis is able to produce large ships for the world market. The Athens–Piraeus area remains, however, much the most important industrial area and attempts to set up equivalent industrial complexes elsewhere have not been very successful.

MUSEUMS

For understandable reasons, museums in Greece are concerned almost entirely with the classical past. There is no national technical museum, no museum of the history of science, no transport museum, no open-air museum. This is because the main concern is the tourist, and all visitors to Greece are assumed to be exclusively interested in scenery, sunshine and the antique, even though, as the Communist countries have emphasised, the natives, resident throughout the year, also have some claim to consideration.

MARBLE QUARRYING

For tourist purposes, the technology of antiquity has been seriously underplayed. In considering the older technological monuments it is natural to begin with the quarries, without which none of the temples and other major attractions offered by the tourist guides could have existed. The most remarkable quarries are at *Mount Pentelikon* (Penteli), 29 kilometres from the Acropolis, which were solely for marble. There are two beds, the lower white and the upper blue-grey. Pentelic marble was greatly prized and much used from 570 BC until Roman times. It takes a good polish and acquires an attractive golden patina as it oxidises. It was used both for the Acropolis and for the Theseion. In general, the architects of classical Greece preferred Pentelic marble and the sculptors Parian. The marble quarries at *Paros* are still in use.

The method of extracting the marble was to cut deep grooves along the edges of the block and then to detach it by driving in wooden wedges. The blocks were then loaded on to sledges, which slid down the Paved Way, held back by ropes passed round bollards along both sides of the roadway. The holes into which the bollards fitted can still be seen.

Other ancient marble quarries can be found in the interior of the island of *Naxos*, between Melanes and Potamia. At Lake Marathon, the artificial lake is held back by what is claimed to be the only marble dam in the world.

Greece

TRANSPORT Canals

There are a number of other examples of ancient technological sites continuing in use until our own times, one of which is the *Corinth Canal* (see plate 4). This was begun by Nero in AD 67, as a means of avoiding the laborious process of dragging ships overland from one side of the isthmus to the other, and the labour force used by Nero's engineers consisted of 6,000 prisoners from Judaea. A large part of the excavation had been completed when the work was stopped by the rebellion of Vindex in Gaul, and the canal was not completed until 1893. It was expensive to build, as 4 of the 6.4 kilometres had to be taken through solid rock, to a depth of 57.7 metres. Technically, the canal was a success, but it is little used by shipping.

TRANSPORT Harbours

In the fifth century BC Themistocles constructed the Long Walls which connected Athens to its outlet on the sea at *Piraeus*. Large sections of the walls can still be seen. There is a Naval Museum in Piraeus, at 38 Philhellinon Street, and the Museum at *Pylos* includes a Naval Historical Museum. The smaller vessels of antiquity had no need of the present large main harbour at Piraeus, but used two semi-circular basins opening south, Zea and Mounychia, the modern *Passalimani* and *Tourkolimano*, where the slipways of the battle triremes are still visible in the rocks. Passalimani has been enlarged and modernised, to take the yachts of the shipping magnates, while Tourkolimano remains small and intimate, with the Royal Yacht Club on its headland.

Another most interesting port is at *Idhra* 257 kilometres from Athens. This was a notorious pirate stronghold in the eighteenth and early nineteenth centuries. A large fleet was based there and much money was made by blockade-running during the Napoleonic wars. Idhra today remains a little old-world port, untouched by the Greek–Turkish wars of 1821–27, a rare phenomenom in Greece. The remains of an abandoned naval ihip-building yard are to be seen at the village of *Mandraki*, where the Miramare Beach bungalow hotel is situated. The holday bungalows are the remodelled dwellings of the workmen who were employed in the once prosperous ship-building yard.

At *Iraklion*, Crete, the modern port is an extension of the original little Venetian port, defended on the north side by a fortress which still stands, and carries the emblem of the winged Lion of St Mark carved in the stone. The Venetians fortified Iraklion in 1206 and converted it into their chief stronghold and naval fort in the Mediterranean. The old walls forming the fortified perimeter are among the longest in the world.

TRANSPORT   Road and Rail

The winding, unmetalled road from *Amphissa*, the chief town in a famous olive-growing area, to *Bralo* (Lamia) has considerable historic significance. It runs for about 40 kilometres and was built by British and French engineers during the 1914–18 war as a means of supplying Salonika by the shortest possible sea route, in order to minimise the threat from submarines in the Aegean and guns on the nearby Turkish coast. The road is now much used by lorries carrying bauxite.

Greece possesses a number of extremely beautiful old stone bridges. Among the most famous are the five-arched bridge at *Arta* (recently spoilt by the building of a new concrete bridge very close by) which is one of the great monuments of medieval Greece; the delicate single-arch bridge over the Agös, near *Konitsa*; the Karytaina bridge in the Peloponnese; and several charmingly proportioned two- and three-arched bridges in the Zagorochia region of Epirus.

Impressive feats of civil engineering were accomplished by the contractor who built the Greek railways. Between *Livadia* and *Lamia–Larissa* both the road and the railway cross northern Phocis and northern Locris. The last section, from the Boeotian Cephis, is one of the most spectacular railways in Europe. Another railway which overcame the problems of a most difficult route was from Diakofton to *Kalavrita*, on the north coast of the Peloponnese. This rack-and-pinion railway runs for 13 kilometres up the ravine formed by the River Bouraikos, to a station at Zachlorni. There are many tunnels and ingeniously sited viaducts, taking the railway from side to side across the river.

AGRICULTURE

Most of the industrial history of Greece is in its fields. One learns a great deal about the traditional economy by visiting the immense olive grove at Delphi, or by travelling along the road from Galata to Poros, which runs through the vast lemon-groves around Lemonodassos, or by touring the district of Chios, with its plantations of gum-mastic trees, or of Edessa in Macedonia, with a large-scale fruit industry, or of Kalamata in the

Peloponnese, famous for its black olives, olive oil and figs. The old agricultural-based industries have, however, been steadily increasing the size of their units. A good example of this is at *Patrai* (Patras); eight kilometres from the centre of the town are the premises and extensive cellars of the Achaia Clauss Winery, which belongs to the Hellenic Vinicultural Company, founded in 1861.

TOBACCO

The tobacco industry is of great importance to Greece, since it provides 30 per cent. of the total value of her exports. There are a number of centres where the buildings and fields belonging to this traditional Greek industry can be studied. *Agrinion,* in Central Greece and *Xanthi, Drama* and *Kavalla* in Macedonia are the more important places; Kavalla has several large nineteenth-century tobacco warehouses.

WINDMILLS

Very charming to look at and of great tourist value, but nowadays of little economic importance, are the many windmills of Greece and Crete. The two best-known concentrations are on the islands of *Mykonos* (see plate 26) and *Crete.* The cylindrical, thatched windmills on Mykonos, with their white, triangular sails, are among the most photographed windmills in the world. Many of them are now half-ruined, but a few, especially along the harbour, have been restored and preserved. The Cretan mills are 75 kilometres east of Iraklion, in the plateau of *Lassithi,* which is dotted with thousands of these small irrigation windmills.

Location of sites - **Greece***

Agös, near Konitsa	40.03N 20.45E	Map 10 CD 56
Agrinion, Central Greece	38.38N 21.25E	Map 10 CD 34
Amphissa, 20 km. from Delphi, on road to Naupailus. Formerly called Salona	38.29N 22.30E	Map 10 DE 34

Arta	39.09N 20.59E	Map 10 CD 45
Bralo (Lamia)	38.55N 22.26E	Map 10 DE 34
Corinth Canal	37.56N 22.55E	Map 10 EF 23
Drama, Macedonia	41.10N 24.11E	Map 9 BC 23
Idhra	37.20N 23.28E	Map 10 EF 23
Iraklion	35.20N 25.08E	Map 10 BC 12
Kalavrita	38.02N 22.06E	Map 10 DE 23
Kavalla, Macedonia	40.56N 20.24E	Map 9 CD 23
Konitsa	40.03N 20.45E	Map 10 CD 56
Larissa	39.38N 22.25E	Map 10 DE 45
Lassithi, east of Iraklion	35.20N 25.35E	Map 10 CD 12
Livadia	41.16N 23.05E	Map 10 DE 45
Mandraki, Idhra		Map 10 EF 23 (no lat. given as Island)
Mount Pentelikon (Penteli)	38.05N 23.53W	Map 10 FG 45
Mykonos	37.25N 25.25E	Island, not on A.A. map
Naxos	37.06N 25.24E	Island, not on A.A. map
Paros	37.04N 25.06E	Island, not on A.A. map
Passalimani		at Piraeus see ref. below
Patrai (Patras)	38.14N 21.44E	Map 10 DE 34
Piraeus	35.57N 23.42E	Map 10 FG 23
Pylos (Navarino)	36.55N 21.42E	Island, not on A.A. map
Tourkolimano		at Piraeus see ref. above
Xanthi	41.07N 24.56E	Map 9 CD 23

* *A.A. Eastern European Handbook, 1970–1*

HUNGARY

In the early eighteenth century the total population of Hungary is estimated to have been less than 4 million. Great areas were unpopulated, and even today this country of 35,900 square miles has only 10 million people, of whom 2 million live in Budapest.

Hungary is not seriously short of natural resources, apart from iron-ore, which is mostly imported from the Soviet Union. It has coal, natural gas, bauxite and manganese. An impressive programme of industrialisation, which has been under way since 1945, has done much to change Hungary from a largely rural and backward country to one in which heavy industry has been developed to an extent which would have seemed impossible 25 years ago, and in which a determined attempt has been made to establish major industrial plants in areas away from Budapest, especially in the eastern regions. There is a serious shortage of manpower, and consequently every attempt has had to be made to install labour-saving machinery and to train the skilled people needed to operate it.

MUSEUMS

Hungary has a number of modern museums which are concerned with industry and technology. The Technical Museum (Müszaki Muzseum) established in 1954 is in *Budapest*, at Kaposvari v.13, Budapest XI. Budapest also has the Transport Museum (Közlekedesi Muzseum, Városligeti körut II, Budapest XIV). The Mining Museum (Bányázati Muzseum) is at *Sopron* (1957) and a specialised museum showing the history and techniques of indigo-dyeing (Kluge Kékfesto–Textilmuzseum) is at *Pápa*

(1962) (see plate 56). This museum is housed in the former Kluge dye-house. The Kluges came to Hungary from Saxony and established their dye-house at Pápa in 1786. It was enlarged in the late nineteenth century and a steam engine was installed in 1905. The works finally closed in 1950, and most of the old equipment has been preserved. The old blast furnace (1813) at *Ujmassa* was reconstructed in 1952 and made the centre of a Museum of Metallurgy. This museum, which is linked to a second museum at Diósgyör, shows the development of the metal industries in the Diósgyör–Hamor region. It also controls five medieval foundries recently excavated in the North and South of Hungary.

TEXTILE INDUSTRY

A good example of the post-war industrial growth is provided by the textile industry at Szeged. The Szeged Textile Works is now one of the largest and most modern textile factories in Central Europe, but it has been entirely constructed since 1950, in an area with practically no previous experience of textiles. Before 1950, most of the mills in Hungary were nearly a century old and their equipment was obsolete. In fact the majority of the machines had been scrapped by British mills and then bought by the Hungarian mill-owners, and even the newer mills could hardly be described as modern. The spinning mill at *Kiskundorozsma*, not far from Szeged, was set up in the late 1930s in the converted stables of a cavalry barracks, with old hand-operated spinning frames made of wood. The old building survives, with its equipment alongside the big new air-conditioned mill, and the contrast between the two symbolises the industrial revolution which has taken place in Hungary within three decades.

The preservation of technical monuments in Hungary has to be seen against this background. A country whose industrialisation has been as recent as Hungary's is not likely to have much in the way of eighteenth- and nineteenth-century monuments, especially when a major war and an internal uprising coming not long afterwards did great damage in the most densely populated areas.

TRANSPORT Bridges

The suspension bridge (Lánchíd) at *Budapest*, a product of the nationalist movement of the early nineteenth century, illustrates this violent and unfortunate sweeping away of history. Previously there had been no permanent link between Buda and Pest; the pontoon bridges had to be broken up each winter, when even the ferry was suspended. The Lánchíd, a chain-bridge with a span of 197.6 metres, was designed by one British engineer, William Thierney Clark, and built under the direction of another, Adam Clark (1866–69). The road tunnel under Castle Hill is also associated with Adam Clark. All the road bridges over the Danube were destroyed by the Germans in 1945, but the towers of the Lánchíd survived and have been used in the new bridge.

Another famous bridge with political associations is the Bridge of Nine Holes (1827), over the River Hortobágy, in eastern Hungary. The *Hortobágy* – the district takes its name from the river – lies between the town of Debrecen and the Tisza river, and is the largest steppe or prairie area in Central Europe. The Bridge of Nine Holes – it has nine regularly spaced arches – is the longest stone bridge in Hungary. By the early nineteenth century the wooden bridge which stood here had become too fragile to carry the growing traffic between Budapest and Debrecen, but for many years permission to build a stone bridge was witheld, because the Imperial authorities in Vienna refused to accept the opinion of the Hungarian engineers that a bridge of this length – 166 metres – could be built of stone. When permission was eventually obtained the bridge was completed in six years.

TRANSPORT Canals and Ship-building

The most important canal in Hungary is the *Sió Canal*, which runs from Lake Balaton to the Danube. The Canal can be more accurately described as the canalisation of the River Sió. The first canal in this system was built by the Roman Emperor, Galerius (293–311), and was maintained during the Middle Ages, but during the Turkish occupation, when transporting grain over long distances was a somewhat perilous occupation, water mills were installed along the Sió. These needed fixed dams and the valley consequently became a marsh. Subsequently, attempts were made to make the Sió navigable again by building sluices, but this did not allow sufficient water to be got away from Lake Balaton; the level of the lake was often still too high and flooding occurred. However, when the railway was built along the southern shore of Balaton in 1858, flood-prevention became urgent. A sluice was therefore built at Siófok, but this proved inadequate and further work was carried out intermittently until the 1950s, when the problem was considered solved.

There has been a shipyard on Lake Balaton, at *Balatonfüred*, continuously since 1846. It has produced mainly small ships for use on Lake Balaton, although some of its ships have been taken elsewhere in Hungary, both overland and via the Sió and the Danube.

WINE-MAKING AND AGRICULTURE

Hungary has extensive vineyards and a large industry based on them. Some of the best known are in the area around Lake Balaton. The grapes for the famous Badacsony Kéknyelü and Szürkebarát wines are grown on *Badacsonyi Hill*. Róza Szegedy's old press house, a fine baroque building, is on the side of this hill. Other press houses and wine-stores, some of the seventeenth and eighteenth centuries, can be seen around *Sárospatak*. Tokay is produced from vineyards on the slopes south of the town. Wine has been made here since Roman times, but the growers who settled in the area in the thirteenth century brought their own vine-stocks with them, and these included stocks of the froment variety.

Another district with a traditional and important fruit-based industry lies on the plateau between the Danube and the Tisza rivers. Large orchards have been developed here and both apricots and apricot brandy are produced, and the main town here is *Keckskemét*. The paprika industry is centred on *Szeged*.

IRON

A place of industrial pilgrimage, despite its comparatively recent foundation, is *Dunaujváros*, the first of the new 'socialist towns' and industrial centres to be established after the change of régime in 1945. Dunaujváros was formerly a fishing village. In twenty years it has grown to be an industrial town of 40,000 people, with the Danube Iron Works as its principal source of employment. It now attracts tourists at the rate of 100,000 a year, all anxious to see where the Hungarian Industrial Revolution began.

A monument of the earlier small-scale iron industry has been preserved at *St Gotthard* (Szentgotthárd), near Rába. This old scythe-forge has been restored, and contains two early nineteenth-century tilt hammers, driven by a waterwheel.

POTTERY AND METAL

Most of Hungary's industrial production now comes from places where a quarter of a century ago there was no industry at all. One should, however, list a few of the older centres where some manufacturing was carried on during the nineteenth century. The Zsolnay porcelain factory at *Pécs* has been in existence for more than 150 years. Another old pottery factory, specialising in majolica, is still in operation at *Hódmezövásárhely*. *Miskolc*, Hungary's second largest industrial city, has possessed a metal-working industry since the middle of the nineteenth century, and now houses the Lenin Metallurgical Works.

MILLS

Hungary has no open-air museum as yet, but some of the smaller technical monuments have been restored and put in the care of local museums. An example of this policy is the *Kiskunhalas* windmill. This brick-built tower-mill, dating from the first half of the nineteenth century, was restored in 1964–66 and is now looked after by the János Thorma Museum.

Another restored mill is at *Ráckeve*. This is a ship-mill, built in the second half of the nineteenth century. The machinery was renovated *c.* 1900 and the whole mill was completely restored 1961–62. It has a paddle-wheel between the 'house-ship' and the store-ship, and is one of the very few ship-mills to survive in Europe out of the many hundred which were operating a hundred years ago.

Location of sites - Hungary*

Badacsony, south of Tapolca	46.48N 17.30E	Map 6	DE 56
Balatonfüred	46.57N 17.53E	Map 6	DE 56
Budapest	47.30N 19.05E	Map 6	EF 56
Dunaujváros	47.00N 18.55E	Map 6	EF 56
Hódmezövásárhely	46.26N 20.21E	Map 6	FG 45
Hortobágy	46.57N 20.38E	Map 6	FG 56
Kecskemét	46.54N 14.42E	Map 6	FG 56
Kiskundorozsma	46.17N 20.04E	Map 6	EF 56
Kiskunhalas	46.26N 19.30E	Map 6	EF 34
Miskolc	48.06N 20.47E	Map 5	DE 23
Pécs	46.04N 18.15E	Map 6	DE 45
Ráckeve	47.10N 18.57E	Map 6	EF 56
Sárospatak	48.19N 21.35E	Map 5	EF 23
Sió Canal	46.23N 18.40E	Map 6	DE 56

St Gotthard	46.58N 16.18E Map 6 CD 56
(Szentgotthárd)	
near Rába	
Szeged	46.15N 20.10E Map 6 FG 45
Ujmassa, north-east of	48.10N 20.42E Map 5 DE 23
Diósgyör	

* *A.A. Eastern European Handbook, 1970–1*

ITALY

Italy does not find it easy to escape from her classical and Renaissance past. With very few exceptions, the museums are devoted to the fine arts and to social and political history prior to the nineteenth century. Despite the efforts of the Commission set up by the Minister of Public Instruction in 1964 to make recommendations on the recording and preservation of historical cultural material, 'monuments', in the Italian context, still means old buildings of great architectural distinction or ruins of the Roman period. 'Industrial monuments' makes poor sense when translated into Italian. Italy has made little attempt, officially or unofficially, to list or preserve her technological monuments, unless they happen to belong to the classical or medieval periods. A good example of the results of this policy can be seen in Venice, where the palaces have been cossetted and the fine eighteenth-century warehouses left to their fate.

MUSEUMS

It is very significant that the national Museum of Science and Technology, in *Milan* (Via San Vittore 21), is called after Leonardo da Vinci and is housed in an old monastery, just as, in a different way, it is significant that the Danish War Museum is in a church.

Only 4.6 million of a total population of 53.6 million now work in agriculture, as over the last 50 years modern Italy has developed as an industrial nation. The old agricultural civilisation has been superbly documented in the large, but strangely inaccessible, Museum of Popular Arts and Traditions (Museo delle Arti e Tradizioni Popolari) in the Quartiere

93

della Esposizione, near *Rome*. This is entirely an indoor museum, and Italy has no open-air museum as such.

There is, unfortunately, no transport or railway museum in Italy. *Turin*, however, has an excellent Automobile Museum, established in 1960, which illustrates the complete history of the Italian motor industry. This museum, the Museo dell'Automobile Carlo Biscaretti di Ruffia, is in a modern building covering 3½ acres. Italy is not, unfortunately, noted for company museums. This is a form of publicity and community service which has made small appeal to Italian industrialists, even in those fields where a strong public relations policy would appear to be good business. An exception to this general rule is the Martini and Rossi Museum at *Pessione*, near Turin, where historic material is blended with encouragement to look favourably on the firm's current production.

Large sections of Italian industry are, however, not covered by museums of any kind, either private or public. The cotton textile industry is a good case in point. This industry was established on a small scale in the fourteenth century and developed on a factory basis in the early nineteenth, when the first spinning machinery was imported from England. It is now of great importance throughout Italy, especially in Lombardy, Piedmont and in the Lucca area of Piedmont. Many of the mills are more than a century old, but no historical survey has been made of them and there is no museum, either for textiles as a whole or for the specialist branches of wool, cotton and silk.

Much the same is true of wine. Italy is the world's largest wine producer; 13 per cent. of the total agricultural area is devoted to grapes, with vineyards spread throughout the entire mainland and on Sardinia, Sicily, Elba, Ischia and Capri. Yet there is only one wine museum of any consequence, the Enoteca Museum of Wine-making in *Siena* (Fortezza Medicea). Again, in Tempio Pausania, Sardinia, the centre of the important cork industry, one might have expected to find an appropriate museum, yet none exists. There is, however, a museum devoted to Italy's most famous national pasta, at the Agnesi spaghetti factory, in *Oneglia*; there is also, perhaps surprisingly, a museum of umbrellas and umbrella-making, in *Gignese*.

TRANSPORT Bridges

It would be absurd to suggest that the technical monuments of antiquity are either uninteresting or unimportant. Italy has, for example, a splendid tradition of bridge-building which goes back for two thousand years. One can instance, at the beginning of this long period, the Ponte Milvio and Ponte S. Angelo in *Rome*, two famous Roman stone bridges which have survived almost in their original condition. In *Florence* the Ponti sull'Arno and the Ponte di S. Trinità were the first examples of stone bridges constructed with a bevelled arch of a new shape, 'basket-handled', to give less resistance to a fast-flowing river. These beautiful and technically important bridges were built between 1566 and 1569. Bartolomeo Ammanati's Santa Trinità bridge was severely damaged during the Second World War, but has been rebuilt exactly as it was, mostly with its original stone, which was dredged up from the bed of the river. In more recent times, there is the iron bridge at *Paderno d'Adda* (1887), which has a span of 150 metres, and the railway bridge over the Isonzo at *Salcano*, a masonry bridge, completed in 1930, with a span of 85 metres. There are a number of covered wooden bridges still surviving. One of the best is at *Bassano del Grappa*, on the edge of the Venetian plain, near the Brenta river. There has been a bridge of this type here since medieval times, but it has been destroyed on a number of occasions, and always rebuilt promptly and accurately. The present bridge dates from 1945.

TRANSPORT Railways

The first railway line to be built in Italy was the 8-kilometre stretch from Naples to Portici (1839). The oldest surviving railway station of any size is Milan – Monza (1840). The Central Station in *Milan*, built by Ulisse Stacchini between 1924–31, is one of the largest in Europe, with a main façade 212.8 metres long (see plate 25). The Porta Nuova station in *Turin* was built in 1865–68 by A. Mazzucchetti. It was seriously damaged during the Second World War, and much rebuilding and restoration has taken place subsequently, but the fine glass roof and bold arch of the original concept still survive.

CIVIL ENGINEERING

The most notable Italian contribution to civil engineering and architecture is the dome. An outstanding early example is to be seen in *Rome*, in the Pantheon, which has survived intact since Roman times, a great tribute to the building. Also in Rome are the domed churches of S. Maria del Fiore, the work of Brunelleschi (1420) and the dome of St Peter's, by Michelangelo (1588–90).

An impressive piece of civil engineering is the curved dam at *Pontalto*, across the narrow gorge of the Felsina, where it discharges into the Adige. The original dam was constructed in 1611, and was raised eight times between 1612 and 1887, as rock built up behind it. A bridge carrying the road from Trento to Povo runs above the dam and is separated from it. The sole purpose of the dam was to protect the valley of the Adige against the fury of the Felsina in times of flood.

MILITARY ENGINEERING

The Italians have also made distinguished contributions to military engineering. An important example in this field is the city-fortress of *Palmanova*. This is surrounded by a wall which includes polygonal bastions, an Italian invention worked out in 1593 by Martinengo and Savorgnan, on behalf of the Venetian Republic. The great Arsenal at *Venice* comes within the same field. Founded in 1104, it is one of the oldest in the world, and now covers 79 acres. Here the great ships of the Republic were built; there were factories for making munitions and weapons, and at the time of the Doges 16,000 men were employed there. A number of the older buildings have been preserved, including the very fine Renaissance-style entrance on the land side, surmounted by the Lion of St Mark, which was designed by Gambella. Adjoining the Arsenal is an excellent Maritime Museum. *Milan* and *Genoa* also have maritime museums.

Another historic dockyard is at *Trieste*, which was established in 1779. The first engineering workshop, L'Officina Meccanica, was set up in 1838, in what had been a prison, and the Arsenal was added to the dockyard in 1853–61. It consisted of a beautiful line of sea-front buildings, including workshops, shipyards and offices. Considerable damage was caused by war-time bombing and shelling btween 1939 and 1944, but parts of the old buildings are still to be seen. The Canal Port in Trieste, which forms an extension of the Porto Vecchio and dates from 1756, should also be visited.

All the major Italian ports were subjected to heavy bombing during the Second World War. By 1945 the port of *Genoa* had been reduced to little more than rubble and scrap iron. The famous old lighthouse in the harbour, the Lanterna di Genova, managed, however, to survive. It was erected in 1139, half-destroyed in 1512 and restored in 1543, and its elegant profile makes it one of the landmarks of Genoa.

METAL AND IRON MINING

By modern standards, Italy's fuel and mineral resources are wholly in-adequate. The need to import most of the raw materials required to keep her industries running makes the national economy somewhat precarious, although a substantial proportion of these imported raw materials are converted into exports of high value, such as motor cars, typewriters, fashion shoes, and the more expensive kind of textiles.

The oldest metal-working site in Italy is at *Campiglia* in Tuscany, where one can see remains of the excavations, slag-heaps and furnaces used by the Etruscans in the production of both iron and bronze. Evidence of much later (eighteenth and nineteenth century) mining and metal working is at *Val Camonica*, near Brescia, where some steel working is still carried on.

Another area with a long tradition of iron-working is *Elba*. The iron deposits here were worked by the Etruscans in the sixth century BC, but the shallow Etruscan workings have by now developed into the large open-cast mines on the coast at Cape Calamita and between Riva Nell'Elba and Cavo, from where lighters towed by tugs carry the ore to the blast-furnaces on the mainland at Piombino.

Very fine examples of iron-construction are to be found in *Milan*, *Naples* and *Genoa*. The great shopping arcade in Milan, the Galleria Vittorio Emanuele (1865), is both an engineering and an architectural master-piece, with its Renaissance façade and great iron and glass roof. Similarly grand arcades are at Genoa – the Galleria Mazzini (1871), and Naples – the Galleria Umberto (1887).

MARBLE QUARRYING

One raw material which does exist in abundance in Italy is marble, much of which is exported. There are famous marble quarries, worked since Roman times, at *Torbole*, and, on a much larger scale, at *Carrara*. A private railway, the Marble Railway (Ferrovia Marmifera) runs for 21.7 kilometres along a precipitous track, from the port (Marina di Carrara) to the quarries at Ravaccione, and visitors can obtain permission to travel on it. There is also a road from the railway station to the Colonnala quarries. Modern quarrying methods, which use explosive to bring down the quarry face, have obliterated nearly all traces of the old quarries, but the station, harbour and roadway still remain as evidence of nineteenth-century workings.

There are many places where nineteenth-century industries have con-tinued and grown in size and importance, without leaving much of architectural or technological interest as evidence of the past. One could instance *Chiavari* in East Riviecera, with the old-established production of slates and chairs, *Savona*, with ironworks and shipyards, *Taranto*, with iron foundries, *Chiampo*, *Pisogne* and *Campione* for textiles and *Ancona*, which specialises in the accordion- and guitar-making industries. Many saw-mills, dating back to the eighteenth and nineteenth centuries, are to be seen in the forested area near *Perarlo Cortina*. Some of the smaller of these mills are water-powered.

Location of sites - Italy*

Ancona	43.37N 13.31E	Map 18 FG 12
Bassano del Grappa, on edge of Venetian plain	45.46N 11.44E	Map 18 DE 45
Campiglia	43.03N 10.37E	Map 26 AB 45
Campione	45.58N 8.58E	Map 18 AB 45
Carrara	44.04N 10.06E	Map 18 BC 12
Chiampo, east of Vicenza	45.33N 11.17E	Map 18 DE 34
Chiavari	44.19N 9.19E	Map 18 BC 12
Elba	42.49N 10.20E	Map 26 AB 45
Florence	43.47N 11.15E	Map 18 DE 12
Genoa	44.24N 8.56E	Map 18 AB 26
Gignese, 8 km. south-west of Stresa, on road to Armeno	45.53N 8.32E	Map 17 FG 45
Milan	45.28N 9.12E	Map 18 AB 34
Naples	40.50N 14.15E	Map 26 EF 12
Oneglia, north-east of Imperia	43.53N 8.02E	Map 17 FG 12
Paderno d'Adda, south-west of Tirano	46.12N 10.10E	Map 18 CD 45
Palmanova	45.54N 13.19E	Map 18 FG 45
Perarlo Cortina	46.24N 12.22E	Map 18 EF 56
Pessione, south of Turin	45.00N 7.40E	Map 17 FG 23
Pisogne, north of Marone	45.48N 10.07E	Map 18 CD 45
Pontalto, east of Trento	46.04N 11.09E	Map 18 DE 45
Rome	41.53N 12.30E	Map 26 CD 23
Salcano, south-west of Gorizia	45.58N 13.32E	Map 18 FG 45
Savona	44.18N 8.28E	Map 18 AB 12

Taranto	40.28N	17.15E	Map 27	EF 34
Trieste	45.39N	13.47E	Map 18	FG 45
Torbole	45.52N	10.52E	Map 18	CD 45
Turin	45.04N	7.40E	Map 17	FG 23
Val Camonica, north of Brescia	45.33N	10.13E	Map 18	CD 34
Venice	45.26N	12.20E	Map 18	EF 34

* *A.A. Continental Handbook, 1970–1*

35 Saltmine pump-rods, Bad Kösen, German Democratic Republic. 1730. The only system of its kind to be preserved. The double rods are driven by a water-wheel. (*see page* 76)

36 Saltworks, Arc-et-Senans, France. *c.* 1770. Building complex. This grand, but commercially absurd project, was the work of Claud-Nicolas Ledoux, Inspector of the Royal Saltworks. The brine was brought by a pipe-line 16 km. long. (*see page* 64)

37 (below) Saltworks, Arc-et-Senans: main entrance.

38 (opposite) Saltworks, Arc-et-Senans: sculpted detail. At a distance, the realistic sculpture can easily be mistaken for salt-incrustations.

39 Luisenhütte charcoal works, Wocklum, West Germany. 1833–34, with subsequent modifications. There were ironworks at Wocklum in the Middle Ages.
The present works were restored in 1958, by the Association of German Engineers. (*see page* 168)

40 Waterdriven nail-maker's forge, Stromfors, Finland. *c.* 1830.

41 Waterdriven forge hammer, Körsan, Sweden. *c.* 1860. The waterwheels which drove these great tilt-hammers have also been preserved. They are 7 m. in diameter. (*see page* 141)

42 Abraham Darby's furnace, Coalbrookdale, England. 1777, incorporating part of an earlier furnace of 1638. The dates of the two furnaces can be seen on the lintels. The 1777 furnace pioneered the use of coal instead of charcoal. (*see page 23*)

43 Iron warehouse, Hargshamn, Sweden. *c.* 1750. This warehouse is on the coast. Iron was stored there during the winter, until the ice thawed and the ships could enter the harbour. (*see page 144*)

44 Clocktower at Kauttua ironworks. Early nineteenth century. (*see page* 59)

45 Iron-workers' houses, Kauttua, Finland.
c. 1800. This ironworking village was
established in the seventeenth century.
The workers' houses shown in the photograph have been restored, together with
a number of other buildings in the village,
by the present owners. (*see page* 59)

46 Administration building of Kauttua ironworks. 1801. This building was also the
owner's residence.

47 Cast iron colonnade, Marianské Lázně, Czechoslovakia. 1889. One of the finest surviving examples of nineteenth-century structural ironwork. (*see page* 46)

48 Spa buildings and exterior of colonnade, Marianské Lázně.

49 Coppermine, Falun, Sweden. The pithead building to the left of centre is *c.* 1720. Copper was first worked here in the eleventh century, and by 1650 this mine was providing most of the copper used in Europe. (*see page* 139)

50 Abraham Pit, Freiberg, German Democratic Republic. 1839. Part of a complex of early-nineteenth century installations which have been preserved to show the development of mining techniques from the sixteenth to the twentieth century. (*see page* 76)

51 Surface installations, Tylorstown Colliery, South Wales. 1900. A typical colliery of the period. The majority of contemporary examples have now been demolished. The building to the right of the pithead gear is a power station, 1912.

52 Mining village, Le Grand-Hornu, Belgium. 1819–40. (*see page* 17)

53 Indigo dyehouse, Pápa, Hungary. 1786, with later modifications. This interesting museum is situated in the former Kluge dyehouse, which was working until
1950. Most of the old equipment has been preserved. (*see page* 87)

54 Limekilns, Stadtlohn, West Germany, 1860. This pair of large, brick-built kilns,
with separate flues, is of an unusual but efficient design.

55 Pulp-beaters, Richard de Bas Papermill, Ambert, France. Mid-eighteenth century. Now preserved as working museum of the handmade paper industry. (*see page* 69)

56 Paper press, Richard de Bas Papermill. The sheets of paper are being stacked as they are removed from the press in which preliminary drying has taken place.

NETHERLANDS

The Netherlands has the second highest density of population of any country in Europe, with only England and Wales ranking higher. This great pressure on space means that each square kilometre has to earn its living; waste cannot be allowed and constant modernisation and rebuilding has been inevitable, even where it was not the result of war-time bombing. Old industrial plants are unlikely to survive, with the exception of windmills, which still do useful work cheaply and have economic value as a major tourist attraction. With the drainage canals, they are the most important element in the 'characteristically Dutch landscape'.

MUSEUMS

Holland is much given to museums, many of which are devoted to aspects of the country's industrial and commerical history. The Railway Museum (Nederlands Spoorwegmuseum, Joan van Oldenbarneveltlaan 6) at *Utrecht* was set up in 1928, based on the collections of G. W. van Vloten, its first administrator. In 1951 it was given a permanent home in the Maliebaan Station (1874), formerly the terminus of the Amsterdam-Hilversum-Utrecht line. The Maliebaan Station was severely damaged during the war and was restored to make it suitable for its new purpose. The Railway Museum is supplemented by the Netherlands Tram Museum at *Weert* (Kruisstraat 6); the National Automobile Museum is at *Driebergen* (2 Buntlaan), and at Schiphol Airport in *Amsterdam* there is the National Aviation Museum.

The Huis Lambert van Meerten Museum in *Delft* (Oude Delft 199) specialises in the history of Delft pottery and tiles – the Delft pottery industry nearly died out in the eighteenth century but there was some revival in the late nineteenth – and the National Glass Museum at *Leerdam* performs a similar service for the glass industry. The Municipal Museum (Stedelijk Museum, Hoogstraat 112) at *Schiedam* incorporates the National Spirits Museum and has exhibits illustrating the history of the gin industry. The National Museum for the Shoe and Leather Industries is at *Waalwijk* (Grootestrant 148) and the Netherlands Textile Museum at *Tilburg* (Gasthuisring 23). There is no mining museum as such, but the museum at *Hoensbroek* has a section devoted to mining.

Somewhat surprisingly, there is no national museum for the history of industry and technology. The National Museum of the History of Science (Rijksmuseum voor de Geschiedenis der Natuurwetenschappen, Steenstraat 1A) in *Leiden* covers part of the field and the Dutch Institute for Industry and Technology in *Amsterdam* (Rozengracht 224–6) has a good collection of more recent material.

One or two of the major industrial concerns have good museums. These include Philips at *Eindhoven*, for the electrical and electronic industry, and van Moppes in *Amsterdam* for the diamond industry. For three centuries, from 1580 onwards, Amsterdam had a world monopoly in the diamond trade, broken eventually by the discovery of diamonds in South Africa and by the rise of a diamond trade in Belgium. After about 1820 there were great changes in the organisation of the Amsterdam diamond industry; diamond cutting and polishing became concentrated in factories, and by 1840 the machinery in most of these factories was driven by steam engines. In 1875 David Levie van Moppes bought No. 16 Plantage Middenlaan and built a big factory there. The four-storey brick building has immense windows, to give the diamond cutters and polishers the best possible conditions for their work, with top-light as well in the uppermost storey. The Company, now known as N.V. Diamant Industrie A. van Moppes & Zoon, has a museum here, containing both a showroom and a workshop.

WINDMILLS

In 1850 there were 9,000 windmills in the Netherlands, and nowadays something like 2,000 are still doing active work, especially in the Zaan area. Winds in the Netherlands are stronger and more reliable than in the eastern part of Britain, and for this reason windmills here found it easier to compete with steam engines.

Mills arouse intense patriotic feeling, as is shown by the establishment in 1952 of the Dutch Foundation for Electricity Generation by Windmills, on the initiative of the Dutch Windmill Society (Vereniging de Hollandse Molen). A number of windmills have been given a new lease of life in this way. They include mills at *Wervershoof* in North Holland, at *Westbroek*, in the Utrecht province, and the fine thatched smock mill, Traanroeier, originally built at Zaandam in 1727 and rebuilt at *Oudeschild* on the island of Texel. Traanroeier began generating electricity in 1965.

There is a very fine mill museum at *Koog aan den Zaan* (Museumlaan 18) 6.4 kilometres north of Zaandam. This houses the collection of the Zaanse Society for the Preservation of Windmills, with examples drawn mainly from the Zaan district, which was started in 1925. The ground floor contains models of mills and exhibits relating to paper-making, while the upper floor has hand tools and apparatus used in the construction and working of mills. The famous Het Pink oil-mill is here, the lower part of which dates back to 1620, the upper part having been rebuilt in 1751, while the reed thatching is about 80 years old. Het Pink was in regular production up to 1933, and was restored in 1939 for preservation as a demonstration mill. Not far away, in Zaandam itself, is the open-air museum known as De Zaanse Schans, which has a collection of Zaan wooden structures, both houses and windmills.

The most notable mill landscape is at *Kinderdijk*, where there are 19 mills within a comparatively small area (see plate 27). Eight were built in 1738, nine in 1740 and two are slightly more recent. The mills are worked on Saturday afternoons during July and August, as a tourist attraction.

Schiedam has two famous windmills. The Drie Korenbloemen (Three Cornflowers) mill, built in 1770 at the end of the old harbour, is still working. The other mill, Walvisch (Whale) is the tallest windmill in the world, with a height of more than 30 metres.

A number of wind and water mills have been preserved at the Open-Air Museum (Het Nederlands Openluchtmuseum) at *Arnhem* (Schelmseweg 89). Among them is the Marten Orges water-driven papermill (early seventeenth century), removed to the Museum in 1933 from the Veluwe, in Gelderen. Also at Arnhem is the Paltrok sawmill from Dordrecht, containing the mechanism invented in the Netherlands in 1592, whereby timber imported from the Baltic could be sawn more quickly and cheaply than by the old hand-saws. This mill was mounted on rollers and could be rotated to suit the wind. The collection at Arnhem includes, too, the early seventeenth-century Bovenkruie cornmill from Delft.

The De Valk Windmill Museum at *Leiden* (Binnenvestgracht 1) has a millwright's workshop, parts of millers' houses and plans and other forms of documentation for different types of windmill. At *Loenen* is the Achterste Molen, a water-driven mill kept running, 'out of piety', by Mr. H. R. Schert, the owner of the nearby modern papermill.

BREWING

Brewing is an important Dutch industry, but most of the buildings in use today are very modern. In *Amsterdam*, the Amstel Brewery was established on its present site in 1870, but there are few traces of the original buildings. Much the same is true of the other major brewery, Heineken's, which took over Amstel in 1968. Heineken was established in Amsterdam in 1868, and is also a major shareholder in the Netherlands' oldest brewery, De Sleutel, at *Dordrecht*, whose history goes back to 1433, and which has some mid-nineteenth century buildings. Only dark beer is brewed here. Historically, the most interesting feature at Heineken is its yeast, the oldest pure yeast culture to be used, without interruption, by any brewery. In the 1880s Heineken followed the advice of Pasteur and made a pure culture of selected yeast cells, which has been used since 1886, and the visitor to the brewery should make a point of enquiring about it and asking to see it.

POLDER DRAINAGE

Much of the Netherlands' history is connected with the struggle against water. The windmills were an essential part of the campaign to prevent flooding and without them much of the Netherlands today would hardly exist. To drain the polders, however, and to add these great areas to the country's usable stock of land, more powerful machinery was needed. The first major project of this kind involved the Haarlemmermeer, which was finally drained in 1852, and of which Schipol airport is a part. The pumping here was carried out by three British-built steam engines, one of which, the Cruquius engine, has been preserved at *Vijfhuizen*, near Haarlem, and has been made the centre of a museum devoted to the history of polder drainage. Part of the museum is in the old boiler-house. The Cruquius station was completed in 1849, and the engine, of 350 hp and built by Harvey of Hayle, worked continuously until 1933, and was saved as the result of efforts by the Royal Institute of Engineers. To avoid disappointment, it should be noted that the Cruquius Museum is closed on Sundays and public holidays, days on which one might well expect it to be open.

A much larger museum in which one can follow the story of the drainage of the polders is the Zuiderzeemuseum at *Enkhuizen* (Wierdijk 13), although this contains no exhibit as spectacular as the Cruquius engine. At Stiedricht, there is a Museum of Dredging. Dredging is an important art in the Netherlands, and boys are trained for it at the Technical School at Stiedricht.

TRANSPORT   Canals and Harbours

The most important modern canal is the North Sea Canal. 24.1 kilometres long, it was opened in 1876. It gave Amsterdam access to the sea at *Ijmuiden,* thereby renewing the prosperity of the city. It is one of the largest ship canals in the world, with a depth of about 15.2 metres. Ijmuiden is now the main Dutch fishing port, with a considerable freight traffic as well. It came into being in 1890, entirely as a consequence of the new canal. The original dam, which gave Amsterdam part of its name, was built in the thirteenth century to provide a sheltered harbour where the little Amstel met the south shore of the river Ij. The dam became a broad square and is now the centre of the city.

Much of the commercial history of the Netherlands is connected with canals, in which a huge investment has been made for many centuries. The Nieuwe Waterweg, cut through to the Hook of Holland between 1866–72, is a good example. It was constructed in order to deal with the problems of silting on the older canal and river outlets from Rotterdam to the North Sea. When it was first built it was only 3 metres deep, but has since been enlarged several times and in that sense the old canal disappeared many years ago.

Port and harbour installations are nearly everywhere new, partly as a matter of policy and partly as a consequence of destruction during the Second World War. An exception is the old harbour, Havik, at *Amersfoort.* Many of the old type of warehouses, with a crane fitted in the centre of the gable, are to be seen along the canals in *Amsterdam,* but the surviving buildings of this date are now only a very small part of the present complex.

TRANSPORT   Railways

Dutch railways were, on the whole, cheap and easy to build, as the land is flat and little was needed in the way of tunnels or elaborate bridges and viaducts. An exception is the great bridge near *Culemborg* (1868), which carries the Utrecht–s'Hertogenbosch line over the Lek (Rhine), with an overall length of 670 metres. It has been restored after war-time damage.

The most important and most impressive station in the Netherlands is Amsterdam Central, built to replace the old Amsterdam Willemspoort station. It was opened in 1889. The oldest surviving station-building is the castle-like structure at *Valkenburg,* on the Maastricht–Aachen line. It dates from 1853.

DAIRY PRODUCE

There are few monuments, other than farm buildings, of one of the Netherlands' major industries, dairy products. At the cheese-centre of *Gouda*, however, the old cheese weigh-house of 1668 was restored in 1959. Cheese is weighed and sold there on Thursday mornings. The town museum, Stedelijk Museum, 'Het Catharian-Gasthuis' (10 Oosthaven), has other material relating to the history of the local cheese industry.

COAL MINING

The Netherlands has a large and efficient coal-industry, in the Limburg area, but there is almost nothing of an archaeological nature to be found there. Although coal had been extracted on a small scale in the Middle Ages, no large exploitation took place before the 1890s, when new private and state mines were established there. The first coal from a state-owned mine came from the Wilhelmina colliery in 1906. The other state collieries, all very big, are Emma (1911), Hendrik (1915) and Maurits (1930). Maurits is the biggest colliery in Europe. The Limburg coalfield is of historical interest mainly because it pioneered the state ownership and direction of coal mines in Europe, symbolised by the palatial headquarters of the State Mines at *Heerlen*.

Location of sites - **Netherlands***

Amersfoort	52.09N	5.23E	Map 10 FG 45
Amsterdam	52.21N	4.54E	Map 10 EF 45
Arnhem	52.00N	5.53E	Map 10 FG 34
Culemborg	51.58N	5.14W	Map 10 FG 34
Delft	52.01N	4.21E	Map 10 EF 34
Dordrecht	51.48N	4.40E	Map 10 EF 34
Driebergen, north-west of Doorn	52.03N	5.17E	Map 10 FG 34
Eindhoven	51.26N	5.30E	Map 10 FG 23
Enkhuizen	52.42N	5.17E	Map 10 FG 45
Gouda	52.01N	4.43E	Map 10 EF 34
Heerlen	50.53N	5.59E	Map 10 FG 23

Hoensbroek, north-west of Heerlen	50.55N 5.55E	Map 10 FG 23
Ijmuiden	52.28N 4.38E	Map 10 EF 45
Kinderdijk, north-north-west of Dordrecht	51.53N 4.38E	Map 10 EF 34
Koog aan den Zaan, north of Zaandam	52.28N 4.49E	Map 10 EF 45
Leerdam	51.54N 5.06E	Map 10 FG 34
Leiden	52.10N 4.30E	Map 10 EF 45
Loenen, north-north-west of Arnhem	52.07N 6.01E	Map 10 FG 34
Oudeschild	53.02N 4.15E	Map 10 EF 56
Schiedam, south-west of Rotterdam	51.55N 4.25E	Map 10 EF 34
Tilburg	51.34N 5.05E	Map 10 FG 34
Utrecht	52.06N 5.07E	Map 10 FG 34
Valkenburg	50.52N 5.50E	Map 10 FG 23
Vijfhuizen	52.21N 5.40E	Map 10 EF 45
Waalwijk	51.42N 5.04E	Map 10 FG 34
Wervershoof, west-north-west of Enkhuizen	52.44N 5.09E	Map 10 FG 45
Westbroek, north of Utrecht	52.09N 5.08E	Map 10 FG 45

* *A.A. Continental Handbook, 1970–1*

NORWAY

Norway is a pleasantly uncrowded country, with only 30 people per square mile, compared with nearly 800 for England and Wales. It has not been an easy matter, though, for this small nation of less than 4 million people to reach its present high standard of living. It is, for the most part, a barren and mountainous country; 73 per cent. of the total area is classed as unproductive and 22 per cent. is forest. Such arable land as there is is found in comparatively narrow strips, gathered in deep and narrow valleys and around fjords and lakes. The forests are one of the chief natural sources of wealth, and industry is based chiefly on raw materials, especially wood, fish, and iron, produced within the country, and on water power – Norway is a very large producer of hydro-electric energy.

MUSEUMS

Norway has a number of excellent museums which contain material of technological interest. The major museum in this field is the Norsk Teknisk Museum, the National Technical Museum, in *Oslo* (Fyrsterkalleen 1). This is a modern museum, established since the war, and it has a good section dealing with the historical development of water-power in Norway. The Folk Museum at *Bygdöy*, Oslo, has brought together more than 150 buildings from various parts of Norway, with the emphasis strongly on the agricultural. At *Lillehammer* is the open-air museum, De Sandvigske Samlinger, which comprises the collection of buildings made by Anders Sandvig at the end of last century and presented to the town in 1900. It includes 48 old workshops, complete with all their tools and equipment, which are in proper working order, so that the old crafts can be demonstrated.

Bergen has four museums which help to tell the story of Norway's industries: the Maritime Museum (Bergens Sjøfartsmuseum); the Museum of the Fishing Industry (Fiskerimuseet); the open-air museum, Gamle Bergen; and the Hanseatic Museum, which illustrates the part played by Bergen in the time of the Hanseatic League. The Hanseatic Museum is on the quay called Bryggen, in two fifteenth-century merchants' houses (see plates 14, 15). The Schötstuene, near the Mariakirke, is also part of the museum; these houses were inhabited by employees of the Hanseatic League, and one of them has been restored.

Other museums of immediate interest are the maritime museums at *Trondheim* and *Oslo*, the Forestry Museum (Norsk Skogbruksmuseum) at *Elverum*, where there is also an open-air museum, as there is too at *Amba*.

Norway is understandably proud of its railways and it is appropriate that the national railway museum (Jernbanemuseet) should be out of the ordinary run of such museums. It is at *Hamar*, in a park on the shore of Lake Mjøsa, close to Hedmark Folk Museum. The Railway Museum covers three hectares and has 400 metres of narrow gauge (750 mm.) railway running through it, together with three old station buildings placed along a standard gauge line. On the first floor of one of these stations, Bestum, is a station-master's flat, furnished in the style of the 1890s.

TRANSPORT   Roads and Railways

Until the coming of railways, transport, away from the coast, was exceedingly difficult. Even now, a high proportion of the road-mileage is not surfaced, and travelling by road in much of Norway needs considerable skill and stamina, even during the summer months.

One gets a good impression of what travelling meant in the days before railways in the Setesdal. From *Moen*, near Björnarå, one can see remains of a perilous-looking road, the Klövvei, which was, until 1870, the only means of communication between the valley and the Bykle.

The railways opened up Norway to an extent which is not paralleled elsewhere in Europe. The first to be built was Oslo–Eidsvoll (1854), a comparatively simple task in comparison with later achievements. The greatest engineering triumph was undoubtedly the Oslo–Bergen line. The 492 kilometres took 26 years to build (1883–1909), and of the 305 kilometres which are over the mountains, 45 are in tunnels and 184 have to be protected by snow-shelters. At its highest point, the line is built at 1,1301 metres above sea-level, and from end to end there are 200 tunnels and 300 bridges.

The Oslo–Bergen road is no less spectacular than the railway. Where it passes through the magnificent scenery of the Måbödal, between *Fossli* and *Sæbo*, it has had to be hewn out of the solid rock, with many tunnels. The engineers who built it had good reason to believe that they were responsible for the most impressive piece of highway construction in Europe.

In the north of the country, the Ofot railway, between the Swedish border and the port of *Narvik*, deserves great respect. It was completed in 1901, to transport iron-ore from the Swedish iron-mines at Kiruna; it runs 230 kilometres north of the Arctic Circle and is the world's most northerly electrified line. It carries 20 iron-ore trains a day, and is kept clear of snow throughout the winter.

Of the many remarkable features to be found on Norwegian railways, we might mention three – an entirely arbitrary selection. *Finse* has the highest station in northern Europe (1,222.4 metres), and on the Sørland railway, beyond *Snartemo*, the line runs through the Kvinsehei tunnel, which is the longest in Norway (5·5 kilometres). The Nordland Railway, beyond *Drevja*, follows the Elsfjörd and the Sörfjörd, and on the most difficult stretch, 5 out of 15 kilometres are taken through tunnels.

TRANSPORT   Canals

Canal builders in Norway had to face almost as great technical problems as the engineers who built the railways. The longest canal is the Telemark Canal (1861–92). It links the towns of Dalen and Skien through a series of lakes. At *Ulefos* boats are raised 54.7 metres through a chain of 15 locks. Another canal with many locks is the Halden Canal, which is 50 kilometres long and provides a route from *Halden* to *Skulerud*.

COPPER MINING

Mining and metal-working have been important in Norway since the seventeenth century. Evidence of the old copper-mining industry is to be found at *Tolga*, where the mines were active from 1670 to 1870, and at *Röros*. Röros Verk was established in 1644, and it was closed in 1921, but subsequently restarted with the aid of a government subsidy. A number of the old timber houses built for the workers at the copper-mine are still to be seen at Röros.

IRONWORKS

The iron industry in Norway was established, largely on the initiative of King Christian IV, in the early seventeenth century, mainly to manufacture cannons and other war material. The first blast-furnace was set up in 1622 at Bærums Verk. Throughout the seventeenth and eighteenth centuries, in Norway as in Sweden, Russia and England, the growth and prosperity of the iron industry were almost wholly dependent on the insatiable requirements of generals and admirals.

In the Ulefos area, near *Holden* on Lake Norsjö, the iron mines were first worked in 1666, but they are no longer in operation. Since 1935 the forges at Holden and Ulefos have belonged to the Cappelen family, whose interests are now mainly in timber and timber products. A similar change from iron to timber took place at *Eidsvoll*, in the Gudbrandsdal. The Eidsvolds Verk dates from the early seventeenth century, and the works and the estate have belonged to the Mathiesen family since 1893. The main building here is of great historic significance in Norway, since it was the meeting place of the National Assembly, which voted the Constitution in 1814.

Another early ironworks is the *Fritzøe Verk*, first established in the seventeenth century and rebuilt in 1850, which continued working until 1951. The *Feiring Jernverk*, another eighteenth-century foundry, was restored 1965–67, together with the old blast furnace.

One of the earliest iron bridges to survive in Norway is at *Fosstvedt*, Holt, a footbridge made in 1836 by the *Naes Jernverk*, one with a long history. During the seventeenth and eighteenth centuries it was well known for its production of cannons. It was modernised between 1799 and 1806 by Thomas Cranford, who came from the famous Carron ironworks in Scotland, and during the nineteenth century produced work of a marvellously high quality, especially in the field of household goods – its beautiful stoves especially are museum pieces.

The fine work which came from Norwegian engineering works and foundries during the nineteenth century has received too little publicity. In the front rank were Kvaerner Brug (1853), which made pumps and engines; Myrens Verksted (1848), which specialised in steam engines; and Thunes Mekanisk Verksted (1815), whose reputation was founded on its locomotives. These three companies, all in *Oslo*, still exist, although their present premises are largely modern.

NICKEL AND SILVER MINING

The nineteenth-century nickel mines at *Evje*, near Kristianar, were abandoned in 1946 and there are buildings and surface equipment to be seen there. At *Kongsberg*, where silver was discovered in 1623, production has continued until the present day, although it has been erratic. In 1814 the ironworks at Kongsberg were transferred into a factory for making armaments and machinery, and are still in use for this purpose today.

GLASS, TIMBER AND BRICK MAKING

A number of Norway's present industrial enterprises have a very long pedigree. The glass works at *Hadeland*, near Jevnaker, 80.5 kilometres from Oslo, was founded in 1762 and is still flourishing. So too is *Halden*, which derives its prosperity from the sawmills set up along the river Tista. The first of these mills began working in the late sixteenth century. The large industrial centre of *Fredrikstad* has a tradition of brickmaking which goes back to the Middle Ages.

Location of sites - **Norway***

Amba	61.10N	8.16E	Map	5 DE 45
Arna, north-east of Bergen	60.25N	5.28E	Map	5 AB 34
Bergen	60.23N	5.20E	Map	5 AB 34
Drevja	66.10N	13.05E	Map	2 AB 12
Eidsvoll, south of Minnesund	60.19N	11.14E	Map	5 EF 34
Elverum	60.54N	11.33E	Map	5 FG 45
Evje, near Kristianar	59.40N	9.36E	Map	7 DE 56
Feiring Jernverk	60.18N	11.10E	Map	5 EF 34
Finse	60.36N	7.30E	Map	5 CD 34
Fossli	60.26N	7.15E	Map	5 BC 34
Fosstvedt	58.38N	8.48E	Map	7 DE 56
Fredrikstad	59.15N	10.55E	Map	5 EF 12
Fritzøe Verk	60.18N	11.12E	Map	5 EF 34
Hadeland, near Jevnaker	60.15N	10.25E	Map	5 EF 34
Halden	59.08N	11.13E	Map	5 EF 12
Hamar	60.57N	10.55E	Map	5 EF 34
Holden	59.15N	9.15E	Map	5 DE 12
Kongsberg	59.42N	9.39E	Map	5 DE 23
Lillehammer	61.06N	10.27E	Map	5 EF 45
Moen, north-west of Björnarå (south of Bykle)	59.18N	7.25E	Map	5 CD 12

Næs Jernverk	58.38N	8.54E	Map 7 DE 56
Narvik	68.26N	17.25E	Map 2 BC 34
Oslo	59.56N	10.45E	Map 5 EF 23
Röros	62.35N	11.23E	Map 4 FG 12
Sæbo, east of Bergen	60.25N	7.07E	Map 5 BC 34
Skulerud, south-east of Oslo	59.41N	11.32E	Map 5 EF 23
Snartemo, north-east of Kvinesdal	58.18N	7.05E	Map 7 BC 45
Tolga	62.26N	11.01E	Map 4 EF 12
Trondheim	63.36N	10.23E	Map 4 EF 34
Ulefos	59.17N	9.15E	Map 5 DE 12

* *A.A. Continental Handbook, 1970–1*

POLAND

The territory now known as Poland has had a turbulent political history and a large part of Western Poland, including the great mining and textile areas of Silesia and the major port of Gdańsk, was under German rule until 1945. Pre-war Poland was primarily an agricultural country, with a low standard of living, whereas Poland today has some of the most important industrial concentrations in Europe. Its agriculture still has a long way to go before it reaches the best European standards, but the steady movement of population into the towns makes thorough-going farm mechanisation inevitable in the near future. The image of Poland as a country of poor peasants is rapidly changing.

MUSEUMS

The development of Polish industry is well documented, both in museums and by careful preservation of those industrial monuments which have miraculously survived the appalling destruction of the war years. In *Warsaw*, there is an excellent Museum of Technology and Industry in the Palace of Culture and Science. *Łódź*, in the centre of the main textile area, has a Museum of Textile History (ul. Piotrkowska 282), now established in the old Gayer factory, and the Museum of Cracow Salt Mines is situated at *Wieliczka* (Park Kingi), close to Cracow, in the galleries of the old salt mines, which date from the eleventh century and are among the oldest and finest in the world. The Maritime Museum is at *Gdańsk* (ul. Szeroka 67–68), the Post and Telecommunications Museum at *Wrocław* (ul. Krasinskiegol). There is an interesting Wine Museum at *Zielona Góra*.

On *Cape Rozewie*, near *Wladyslawowo*, is the Stefan Zeromski lighthouse, the most powerful on the Baltic, which houses a lighthouse museum. Similar museums in industrial monuments are to be found at *Duszniki* (ul. Klodzka 42), where the core of the museum is an historic paper-mill and, at *Krosno*, where there is what is well described as a 'reserve' of the petroleum industry. The policy in Poland is to establish a network of technical museums of this kind, with the aim of creating a popular interest in the development of technology, although the difficulties of preservation are not underestimated. An inventory of the more important technological monuments, drawn up soon after the new Historic Monuments law of 1962, has so far produced nearly 1,500 monuments which are considered worthy of scheduling and preservation.

This inventory is, in effect, a selection of the great catalogue built up during the past twelve years by the Institute for the History of Material Culture (Instytut Historii Kultury Materialnej) on behalf of the Polish Academy of Science. No other country has so far produced anything to equal this catalogue. Every monument is recorded and photographed district by district. This survey has been made by small teams of specialists. In the case of mining, the three-man research group was made up of experts in the history of mining, in mining technology and in industrial buildings. This allowed a complete and authoritative record to be made of both the underground workings and the surface installations, together with any associated buildings in the neighbourhood, such as workers' housing.

MINING AND METAL WORKS

Poland is rich in mineral resources, which have been exploited for many centuries and it is natural, therefore, that particular attention should have been given to the history and archaeology of mining. Nine sites or groups of sites have so far received detailed investigation. They are:

1. The quartz mines at *Krzemionki Opatowske*. These were chosen as being the best preserved of the 43 neolithic mining sites in Poland.
2. The haematite mines at *Rudki*, which date from the second to the fourth century AD
3. The lead and silver mines at *Olkusz*. These mines belong to the thirteenth and fourteenth centuries.
4. The salt mines at *Wieliczka*, which have already been mentioned above and which were in operation from the thirteenth century until comparatively recently.
5. Surviving evidence of mining and iron-working (sixteenth-twentieth centuries) near *Olkusz*.

6. The lead and silver mines at *Tarnowskie Góry*, which were worked from the sixteenth until the nineteenth century.
7. Surviving evidence of mining and iron-working in the *Tatry mountains* and near *Nowy Sacz*, also sixteenth to nineteenth centuries.
8. Similar sixteenth–nineteenth century remains at *Iłża, Kielce, Końskie* and *Kraków*.
9. Stone quarries, dating from the eleventh century onwards, at various places. These include two marble quarries near *Kielce* and other marble quarries at *Chęciny*.

A few industrial monuments have survived in reasonably good condition without the expert attention of government departments. Skarzysko-Kamienna is an important modern centre of the metallurgical industries and nearby is *Wachóck*, where ironworking has existed since the Middle Ages. The present buildings date from 1833.

Several other iron-working complexes which were important in the nineteenth century have been preserved, a number of them on the extreme western side of the Iłża district. The great rolling-mills at Sielpia Wielka, south-east of *Konspie*, date from 1821. This Swedish-type industrial settlement contains workers' houses, a hospital, a school and an administrative building. The mills were water-powered and much of the original plant survives. At Parszów, north-east of Końskie, there has been metal-working since the sixteenth century. The present buildings date from 1748. The water-driven blast-furnaces and hammers at Stara Kuźnica, east-north-east of Końskie, date from 1838, although there were ironworks here in 1662. Bzin, north-west of *Starachowice*, has a blast-furnace building of 1823.

Another interesting industrial settlement is at Bialogon, west of *Kielce*. The main development here was during the first half of the nineteenth century and the present buildings, which include workers' housing and rolling-mills, belong to this period. Bobriza, north-north-west of *Kielce* and west of Samsonow, has early and mid-nineteenth century blast-furnaces and workers' houses.

All these early Polish iron-works in the Kielce and Iłża districts were on rivers. There are a great many of them, mostly in a ruinous condition or mere sites on a map. Those mentioned here were of exceptional size and importance and have survived in a reasonable state of preservation until modern times.

The most notable is at *Samsonow*, one of the earliest industrial townships in Poland. It supplied arms to the Polish kings from the early seventeenth century. The original foundry and workshops were built and organised by an Italian named Cacia, from Bergamo, who set up the first blast furnace here. The premises were destroyed during the Swedish wars of the seventeenth century and rebuilt in the early nineteenth century. The site has been carefully restored and preserved as a national monument. A museum of the industry of the Kielce province has been set up at Sielpia.

MILLS

Zyrardów is named after the Frenchman, Philippe Girard, the inventor of a pioneering spinning machine. Girard established the first Polish spinning mill here. At their peak, the mills at Zyrardów employed 10,000 workers and were one of the biggest textile complexes in the world. The original mills have gone, but some of the old weavers' houses have survived. Other weavers' houses have been preserved at Chelmsk (early eighteenth century) and at Łódź (early nineteenth century).

The Great Mill (Wielki Mlyn) at *Gdańsk* was built by the Teutonic Knights in the mid-fourteenth century, on the Radunia Canal (see plate 34). In its day, this seven-storied grain mill, which had nine millstones, was the most imposing industrial building on the shores of the Baltic. The Great Mill was severely damaged during the 1939–45 war, but was restored in 1962 and is now preserved as a national monument. At *Kazimierz Dolny* there are several sixteenth-century granaries. One, in Krakowskie Przedmiescie Street, has been converted to make a tourist hotel and consequently appears safe against threats of possible demolition.

TRANSPORT   Canals

There are two especially interesting canals in Poland. The *Augustow Canal* (Kanal Augustowski) joins the river Vistula to the Neem, and was completed in 1844. The *Elblag Canal* (Kanal Elblaski) which runs through the western part of Mazuria, contains a noteworthy technical feature: to avoid the use of locks, ships and barges are hauled over a stretch of dry land by means of five separate sets of electrically-driven winches.

Location of sites - **Poland***

Augustow Canal	52.51N 23.00E	Map 3 EF 45
Cape Rozewie	54.50N 18.20E	Map 3 BC 56
Checiny	50.49N 20.28E	Map 5 DE 56
Dusniki, south-east of Klodzho	50.27N 16.39E	Map 5 CD 45

Elblag Canal (Kanal Elblaski)	54.10N	19.25E	Map	3 CD 45
Gdańsk	54.22N	18.41E	Map	3 BC 56
Iłża	51.11N	21.13E	Map	5 DE 56
Kazimierz Dolny, west of Lublin	51.20N	21.56E	Map	5 EF 56
Kielce	50.51N	20.39E	Map	3 DE 12
Końskie	51.12N	20.23E	Map	5 DE 56
Kraków	50.03N	19.55E	Map	5 CD 45
Krosno	49.40N	21.46E	Map	5 EF 45
Krzemionki Opatowskie	51.44N	18.12E	Map	3 BC 23
Łódź	51.49N	19.28E	Map	3 CD 23
Nowy Sącz	49.39N	20.40E	Map	5 DE 45
Olkusz	50.18N	19.33E	Map	5 CD 45
Rudki, south-east of Glogów	51.31N	16.17E	Map	3 AB 12
Samsonow	50.52N	20.39E	Map	5 DE 56
Starachowice	51.03N	21.00E	Map	5 DE 56
Tarnowskie Góry	50.28N	18.40E	Map	5 CD 56
Tatry mountains	Approximately 49.27N	12.17E	Map	5 CD 34
Wachóck	51.07N	21.00E	Map	3 EF 12
Wieliczka	50.00N	20.03E	Map	5 CD 45
Wrocław	51.05N	17.00E	Map	3 AB 12
Zielona Góra	51.57N	15.30E	Map	2 EF 23
Zyrardów	52.02N	20.28E	Map	3 DE 23

* *A.A. Eastern European Handbook, 1970–1*

PORTUGAL

The Portuguese deposits of iron, copper, tin and gold were exploited by the Romans. They excavated to a depth of 100 metres, and these mines, made with a total disregard for life and safety, are still to be seen. The iron mines were worked in the eighteenth and nineteenth centuries, but on no great scale.

A landmark was the granting of the first mineral concession, in 1823, for lead mining at Braçal and Malhada, followed by others for tin and antimony in 1839. Between 1850 and 1900 no fewer than 324 mines were concessioned – tin, lead, copper, antimony, manganese, gold, iron, wolfram, chrome, molybdenum, zinc, all in the region of *Malhada* and *Guarda*. Radium and uranium followed in 1909, with refineries at Guarda, Barracâo and Urgerrica.

These mineral resources are still, however, under-exploited. The story of Portugal's industries is largely told by her export figures. In 1967, the leading exports were cork, wine and sardines. In the next three places, but a very long way behind, were pulpwood, resin and olive oil. Strenuous efforts are being made to broaden the base of the economy by encouraging investment in manufacturing industries, but, outside the four main areas – Lisbon, Oporto, Braga and Aveiro, the impression Portugal still gives to a visitor is that of a predominantly agricultural, rural country. This is, of course, good for tourism, which, in 1967, brought in more foreign currency than all the exports combined.

Some of the newer agriculture-based industries are now of considerable economic importance. One of the largest, tomato concentrate, is less than 40 years old. The first factory was set up in 1938, in the province of Ribatejo. There are now more than 20 such factories.

MUSEUMS

Portugal has no museum of science and technology, no open-air museum and very few company museums. The emphasis in museums is on the art treasures, the wealth and the maritime and colonial power of Portugal's great past, which was, however, quite a long time ago. There are, nevertheless, pointers to what might happen during the next ten years. More industrial concerns may, one hopes, follow the example of Vista Allegri, the great porcelain works, founded in 1824, near *Aveiro*, where there is a works museum and the factory, too, can be visited.

Among the specialist museums which have been proposed are those for mining (possibly near the mines of São Domengo), for cork, and for the sardine industry; there is a museum for port wine in *Lisbon* (rua S. Pedro de Alcantura 45), and another for wine is planned in Oporto. All these would have attractions for tourists, as would a transport or railway museum, which might be conveniently and appropriately situated at one of the older and more distinguished railway termini, such as the S. Bento in *Oporto*, the Estação do Rossio, with its Moorish façade, in *Lisbon* (see plate 24), or *Viana do Castelo*. The railway workshops at *Barreiro* include the offices of the original Barreiro station of the Southern and South-western Railway, a single-storey building (1859) by P. and W. MacLellan of Clutha Iron Works, Glasgow.

An open-air museum in Portugal would still have much material on which to draw, although the problem of collecting items in good condition becomes more difficult each year. One thinks, for instance, of the windmills along the valley near São Tiago de Cacem and wonders what their condition will be in five or ten years from now.

WINE INDUSTRY

The wine industry has a number of interesting monuments. *Vila Nova da Gaia*, the Roman Cale, on the left bank of the Douro, is the main storehouse for wines from the Upper Douro, the so-called port wines. The wine is brought in casks to the wine lodges at Vila Nova in April, and is left there for maturing and blending and eventual shipment abroad. The port-wine lodges mostly date from the late eighteenth century, and are attractive whitewashed buildings, with arched colonnades along the front. The pipes of port are stacked inside, up to four high. *Coimbra*, too, has a number of important wine lodges.

At *Oporto* itself, the British Factory House (1785) illustrates the long and close links between England and Portugal. The Factory House, whose members were drawn from the numerous port-wine firms, was a combination of club, exchange and depot.

Fine cellars of the more traditional type are to be seen at many places within the wine-growing areas, and there are some particularly notable examples around *Bussaco*.

SHIP-BUILDING

Portugal's old naval traditions are mostly documented in books and museums, and they have left little in the way of archaeology. The Naval Museum in the old palace of the Count of Farrobo, at Alferte, near Lisbon, contains a large amount of material relating to ships, navigation, commanders, campaigns and life at sea, but little relating to ship-building. At *Lagos* one can see the bay where Prince Henry the Navigator had his shipyards, but only the site survives.

A modern port had been planned for *Lisbon* for more than 200 years. In 1755, the future Marquis of Pombal commissioned Carlos Mardel to draw up a plan for the development of the port of Lisbon, to be based on the construction of a naval yard which would, at that time, have been the largest in the world. The shipyard remained no more than a pipe dream however, and nothing practical was in fact done until the 1960s. Since 1962, a large shipyard has been built on the south bank of the Tagus in Margueira Bay, capable of taking the biggest ships in service. Between this new yard and the wharves and jetties of the eighteenth and early nineteenth centuries there is a very considerable gap. Anyone in search of nineteenth-century ports, dockyards and warehouses will find little to catch his attention in Portugal, although there are many pleasant and picturesque small ports and harbours and the occasional curiosity, such as the seventeenth-century port of St Teodusio, at *Sesimbra*, not far from Lisbon, which is now little more than a lighthouse.

BRIDGES AND AQUEDUCTS

Portugal displays a considerable continuity of achievement in bridges, viaducts and aqueducts. One of the best early aqueducts is near *Lagos*, on the Rossio da Trinidade. It was built between 1490 and 1520 to bring water to the town of Lagos, which it still does. Two of the nineteenth century's most impressive iron bridges are in Portugal; one is an early steel bridge, the Maria Pia bridge (1877) at *Lisbon* designed jointly by the great French engineer Gustave Eiffel and T. Seyrig and the other is the Dom Luis I bridge over the Douro at *Oporto* (see plate 10) by Seyrig. The modern suspension bridge (1966) over the Tagus at *Lisbon* takes its place in the series.

There are a number of important nineteenth-century bridges which were built to carry the railway over major rivers. From an engineering point of view the most interesting are those spanning the river Douro at *Oporto, Ferradosa* and *Barca d'Alva*; across the river Lima at *Vianodo Castelo*; the Guardiana at *Moura*, the Tagus at *Praia do Ribatejo* and *Abrantes*.

SALT PRODUCTION

Salt production is carried on at a number of places. At *Aveiro* there are lagoons used as salt marshes, where large pyramids of salt pile up during the summer. The canal from the town to the coast has a strangely formal appearance, emphasised by the obelisks placed along it. Near *Vila Real de Santo Antonio* there are the salt marshes of Castro Marim Pomarão, and a further extensive series is to be found along the river Sado, near *Setúbal*, the principal centre of the sardine-canning industry.

Location of sites - **Portugal***

Abrantes	39.28N	8.12W Map 23 BC 45
Aveiro	40.38N	8.40W Map 19 AB 12
Barca d'Alva	41.01N	6.57W Map 19 CD 23
Barreiro	38.40N	8.40W Map 23 AB 34
Bussaco, north of Coimbra	40.23N	8.22W Map 23 BC 56
Coimbra	40.12N	8.25W Map 23 BC 56
Ferradosa, Oporto	41.06N	6.57W Map 19 AB 23
Guarda	40.43N	7.17W Map 23 DE 56
Lagos	37.05N	8.40W Map 23 AB 12
Lisbon	38.44N	9.08W Map 23 AB 34
Malhada, south of Guarda	40.32N	6.55W Map 23 DE 56
Moura	38.08N	7.27W Map 23 CD 23
Oporto	41.09N	8.37W Map 19 AB 23
Praia do Ribatejo	38.26N	8.20W Map 23 BC 45

Sesimbra	38.26N	9.06w	Map 23 AB 34
Setúbal	38.31N	8.54w	Map 23 AB 34
Viana do Castelo	41.42N	8.50w	Map 19 AB 34
Vila Nova da Gaia, left bank of Douro	41.08N	8.37w	Map 19 AB 23
Vila Real de Santo Antonio	37.12N	7.25w	Map 25 AB 67

* *A.A. Continental Handbook, 1970–1*

RUMANIA

Rumania is a country with immense natural resources, but its industrial development was very slow until after the Second World War. The reasons were largely political – Turkish occupation until the 1830s, a weak monarchy and a series of corrupt governments until the end of the 1930s, dependence on foreign capital, German occupation during the 1940s, war-time devastation, and a poor education system. As elsewhere in Eastern Europe, a remarkable change has taken place during the past twenty years. In Rumania, the volume of industrial production in 1968 was ten times what it was in 1938. In 1939 only 5 per cent. of the machinery and equipment needed by its industries was produced at home, but the proportion has now risen to 65 per cent.

MUSEUMS

The small-scale, village-type production of the eighteenth and nineteenth centuries is excellently documented at the Village Museum at Herăstrăv Park (Soseaua Kiseleff 28–30), near *Bucharest*. Established in 1936 it covers 22 acres, and now contains more than 200 buildings skilfully distributed over the site, in such a way that one has the feeling of being in a real village rather than an open air-museum. The exhibits include windmills from North Dobruja, a small building for processing and preserving fish from the Danube delta, a mill from the Motzi region for crushing gold-bearing rock, and an iron-foundry. Also in Bucharest is the Technical Museum at Str. Candiauŏ Popescu 2, while part of the Ethnographical Museum of Transylvania takes the form of an open-air museum at *Cluj* (Str. 30 Decembrie 21).

A separate open-air museum for later technological material is being developed at Sibiú, and at *Ploiesti* there is a museum devoted to the oil industry. It was established in 1960. The Museum for Agricultural Technology is at *Dumbrava Sibiului*, and its collections necessarily overlap to some extent with those of the Village Museum, particularly in the case of windmills and watermills.

WATERMILLS

In the past the Rumanian peasants made great use of watermills. These have been carefully studied and in many cases restored and preserved, either on their original sites or in open-air museums. Two types of mill were in use, one with a horizontal wheel and the other with a vertical wheel, the first type providing the simplest kind of cereal mill and most frequently found in the hilly country near the Carpathians, an area of small, fast-running streams. The faster the flow, the shorter the distance from mill to mill. Water was brought to the wheel by means of hollowed half-trunks of trees, by an open board trough, or by a penstock.

The mills with vertical waterwheels were set up either on the river bank or floating in the river, with the large undershot waterwheel fixed between two boats. There are now only eight of these boatmills left, on the rivers Olt, Mureş and Gomeş; they need frequent repair and have to be protected from damage by floating ice.

RAILWAYS

Rumania, like Greece, was a difficult country in which to build railways, and, with the poor freight potential in the nineteenth century, it was not easy to find investors willing to provide the necessary finance. Consequently Rumania constructed its railways comparatively late. Their history is illustrated at the Railway Museum in *Bucharest*, which is housed in part of the Northern Station (1870). This is the oldest of Rumania's surviving termini. It has been extended several times and was restored in 1944, after wartime damage.

SALT MINES

Among the most interesting industrial monuments in Rumania are the salt mines. At *Slănic*, north of Ploiesti, there are a number of mines which have been worked since the seventeenth century, and near *Baia Bacului* there is an open-cast salt mountain, rightly designated one of Rumania's natural monuments. At *Ocna Dejuliu* the large salt mines have been worked continuously since Roman times; they are shallow, with seams of only 21.3 metres, and they include an underground salt-mill.

METAL MINING

At *Oravița* one can see traces of the gold, silver and iron mines which were worked by the Romans. Another very old metal-working site is at *Hunedoara*, where the iron industry is mentioned as early as the thirteenth century. In the second half of the nineteenth century Hunedoara became an important industrial centre, with blast-furnaces to process iron-ore from the mines of *Gherla* and *Telciu*, mines which were in operation in the second and third centuries. New open-hearth furnaces have been installed since 1945, but there is still some evidence of the older plant, more especially in subsidiary buildings.

OIL REFINING

One of the first oil refineries in the world was built at *Ploiesti*. Production was first recorded in industrial statistics in 1857, when the original distillery, yielding 250 tons a year, was commissioned at Rîfov, near Ploiesti, to supply kerosene to Bucharest for street lighting. The installation at Ploiesti and much of the town was almost entirely destroyed during the Second World War, and virtually everything one sees there now outside the Museum is entirely modern. Of the national investment 21 per cent now goes to the oil and natural gas industries, with deposits exploited over a much wider area.

CONCRETE

At *Brăila* on the Danube, however, a different kind of nineteenth-century industrial pioneering has met with better fortune. In 1888–89 the Rumanian engineer Anghel Saligny built a group of grain-stores here, using prefabricated concrete panels. So far as can be discovered, this was the first time this technique, widely used today, was employed anywhere in the world.

WINE MAKING

Rumania has produced wine for many centuries – the vineyards at *Drăgășani*, east of Rîmnicul Vilcea, go back two thousand years to Dacian times – but the buildings used for processing the grapes were largely of wood and are mostly of little antiquity or interest. There are, however, two monuments associated with the wine industry which deserve special mention. At *Alba Iulia* in the great citadel, which was built with serf-labour between 1715 and 1738, part of the extensive underground network of casemates, tunnels and passages is now used by the state wine and spirit enterprise, Vinalcool. North of Alba Iulia, at *Telna*, there is a majestic eighteenth-century wine cellar, 152 metres long, which was also dug by serfs. It is open to visitors.

Location of sites - **Rumania***

Alba Iulia	46.04N 23.33E	Map	7 CD 34
Baia Bacului	47.38N 23.44E	Map	7 CD 45
Brăila	45.17N 27.58E	Map	15 BC 23
Bucharest	44.25N 26.07E	Map	7 EF 12
Cluj	46.47N 23.37E	Map	7 CD 45
Drăgăşani	44.40N 24.16E	Map	7 DE 23
Dumbrava Sibiului (Sibiú)	45.46N 24.09E	Map	7 DE 34
Gherla	47.02N 23.55E	Map	7 CD 56
Hunedoara, south of Eleij	45.45N 22.54E	Map	7 CD 45
Ocna Dejuliu	47.08N 23.55E	Map	7 CD 45
Oraviţa	45.02N 21.43E	Map	7 BC 23
Ploiesti	44.57N 26.01E	Map	7 EF 23
Slănic, north of Ploiesti	45.14N 25.58E	Map	7 EF 23
Telciu	47.25N 24.24E	Map	7 DE 56
Telna, north of Alba Iulia	46.08N 23.33E	Map	7 CD 34

* *A.A. Eastern European Handbook, 1970–1*

SPAIN

There is no reason why Spain should not have become one of the major industrial powers of Europe; it was prevented from doing so, however, during the nineteenth century by a political and religious system which forced the country to live to an altogether unreasonable extent in the past, with disastrous effects on the standard of living of the mass of the people. The result is that agriculture is still the main source of livelihood – four people work in agriculture, forestry and fishing, for every three employed in manufacturing – and the country's natural resources are far from adequately exploited. On the other hand, considerable efforts have been made during the past 20 years to secure a more reasonable investment in industrial development and modernisation and to improve technical and scientific education, which is nearly as poor as in Greece. There is considerable leeway to be made up at the lower levels of education, too: in 1960, 14 per cent. of all persons aged 10 or over could neither read nor write.

The present situation is that the province of Barcelona accounts for 20 per cent. of Spain's industrial production, including 75 per cent. of its textile capacity and 60 per cent. of its metallurgy. Barcelona is the driving force behind the most progressive and most prosperous region of Spain, Catalonia, which comprises the provinces of Barcelona, Gerona, Lérida and Tarragona. In Catalonia as a whole, nearly half the working population is engaged in manufacturing industry. Much of this industry, however, is carried on in very small units, as a walk through the older parts of Barcelona will make clear.

MUSEUMS

There is no national museum of industry or technology, but there are good shipping museums at *Barcelona* (Museo Marítimo de Barcelona, Reales Altarazanas) and *Madrid* (Museo Naval, Montalban 2). The Museo de Industrias y Artes Populares in Madrid covers the older, handicraft-type industries. There is also a Geological and Mining Museum in Barcelona, in the Parque de la Ciudadela.

CIVIL ENGINEERING

Spain, like Italy and France, contains a number of well-preserved master-pieces of Roman technology, and one of the most remarkable is the aqueduct at *Segovia*, known as El Acueducto (see plate 1), which was built *c*. AD 80 and is one of the peaks of Roman engineering. It has two tiers of arches, each with a span of 4.6 metres, the bases of which are only 2.4 metres wide and the granite blocks are so accurately dressed that they remain in position without either mortar or clamps. The total length of the aqueduct is 820 metres. It was restored by Queen Isabella in the fifteenth century, to bring water to the city from the Sierra Guada-marra, 16 kilometres away. Another fine Roman aqueduct is at *Tarragona*, the Acueducto de las Ferreras, which also has two rows of arches.

At *Alcántara* is the great bridge built at the order of the Emperor Trajan. Its piers are of granite and arches 28 metres wide carry the road-way at a height of more than 50 metres above the river. The stones form-ing the arches weigh up to 8 tons each and are fitted without cement.

Much interesting work in the construction of dams was carried out in Spain. The principle of the reservoir dam was introduced into Spain by the Romans. The two finest surviving examples of Roman dams are at *Mérida*, near the Portuguese frontier. They were originally built to pro-vide a water supply and they are still in use, although nowadays for irrigation purposes. The two dams, the Prosperina and the Cornalvo, are built of masonry and concrete, with considerable amounts of earth fill.

Among the later dams is that at Almonacid de la Cuba, near *Belchite*, in Aragon. In its original form it was a straight, massive wall built across a deep gorge, but it was later heightened, in an attempt to defeat the silting which had made it useless as a reservoir. This effort failed, and nowadays the reservoir is full to the top with soil and under cultivation.

At the end of the fourteenth century the *Almansa* dam was built in the province of Albacete. It was raised in 1586. The original wall, the bottom part of the dam, is curved. So too is the much larger *Alicante* dam (1579–

94) on the River Monegre. It was an enormous structure for its time. For 300 years after it was built it remained the highest dam in the world.

In the seventeenth century large curved dams continued to be built, but they were of a much more slender construction. The most important examples are those at *Elche* and at *Relleu*, on the river Amadorio.

In 1747 the prototype of all modern buttress dams was built near *Almendralejo*, in Badajoz. This dam was constructed to drive milling machinery. The millstones and the waterwheel which drove them were placed actually within the body of the dam, the first time this is known to have been done. The designers of Almendralejo were pioneers twice over.

TRANSPORT   Railways

Much of Spain is mountainous and railway building has involved a great many bridges and tunnels, some of which are very impressive. Two of the most difficult stretches of lines to build were the Puerto de Pajares, in the Asturias, and the Puerto del Manzanel, in Galicia. On the first of these, between *Busdongo* and *Puente de los Fierros*, the line descends 731 metres in the course of 41 kilometres and on the second, the most spectacular stretch is between *Brañvelas* and *Ponferrada*. Both of these lines were completed in the early 1880s.

The first railway in Spain, from Barcelona to Mararó, dates from 1848. Development was slow until 1855, but between then and 1870 more than 4,800 kilometres were built, largely with foreign capital. Many of the most remarkable engineering achievements belong to this period, among them the viaduct at *Ormaiztegui*, Guipúzcoa, on the main line from Madrid to Irún (1864), which was damaged during the Civil War. Another noteworthy viaduct, completed in 1866, crosses the river Guadiana and carries the line from *Ciudad Real* to *Badajoz*. The most famous tunnel is the *Argentera*, 144.8 kilometres from Barcelona, on the line to Zaragoza. This tunnel was begun in 1883, but, as a result of financial and technical difficulties, was not in service until ten years later.

The oldest railway station is the Atocha station in *Madrid* (1851), built to serve as the terminus for the line to Aranjuez. The original buildings have been considerably enlarged.

A small railway museum (Museo del Ferrocarril) was established in Madrid in 1967. The emphasis at present is on models and other small items, but it is hoped that a new site will be found shortly, to allow original locomotives and rolling stock to be preserved and displayed. The Museum has, however, been placed in a somewhat ridiculous position. Two thirds of the Spanish railways are broad-gauge. The remaining third, which are of the standard European gauge, were nationalised in 1941 and are run by a board known as R.E.N.F.E. (Red Nacional de Ferrocarriles Españoles). The railway museum was established by R.E.N.F.E., which is only a minority shareholder, so to speak, in the railways of the country. The broad-gauge itself is a curious piece of archaeology. It has been kept different from that of its immediate neighbours, France and Portugal, for what are called strategic reasons, i.e. the defence of the country against military attack. Passengers consequently have to change trains at the frontier stations, a cause of inconvenience which is successfully by-passed by the aeroplane.

WINE

The best wine museum, at Villafranca del Panades near *Barcelona*, includes a fine collection of old wine-presses. The wine firm, Torres, of Villafranca, has some of the oldest cellars in the region, with enormous wooden vats, one of which holds 500,000 litres. At *San Sadurni de Noya*, near Barcelona, the huge wine cellars can be visited. They are claimed, possibly correctly, to be the biggest in the world. *Jerez* is the centre of the sherry trade and contains the headquarters of a number of large shippers. Chief among these firms are Gonzalez Byass and Williams and Humbert, both of whom occupy pleasant eighteenth-century buildings. Jerez has a number of bodegas – open-fronted store-houses – of the same period (see plate 65). So, too, has *Tarragona*, where the bodegas are rather larger than at Jerez. Tarragona has another claim to alcoholic distinction, for the monks expelled from the Grande Chartreuse in France have made their famous liqueurs here since 1903.

SHIPBUILDING

Shipbuilding is an old-established industry in Spain. For civil purposes, the main dockyards are at *El Ferrol* and *Cartagena*. Some buildings and installations of the second half of the nineteenth century are to be seen at each of these two yards, although most of the premises and equipment are much more recent. The chief naval yards are at Barcelona, Bilbao, Seville and Cadiz. The Museo Histórico Municipal in *Cadiz* tells the story of the city as a port.

TEXTILES

The manufacture of cotton and woollen goods has been important for more than a century, especially in Catalonia. The principal towns involved in the textile industry are in the Barcelona area. They include *Badalona* and *Tarrasa*. At *Bejar* a few of the mills, still in operation, are of the older three- and four-storeyed type. Spain has the lowest domestic consumption of textiles per head of any Western European country, except Portugal, but the production of synthetic fibres, mainly for export, has developed rapidly since the mid-1960s. Spain is now ahead of Belgium, Austria, Sweden and Switzerland in this respect, and takes sixth place in Western Europe. Many of the new factory buildings to be seen in Catalonia are for the production of textiles based on synthetic fibres.

COAL AND IRON

Coal and iron are extensively mined in the north of the country, especially around *Barcelona*. There is, however, no museum which is concerned with mining as such, although in Barcelona the Museo de Geologia has fine collections of the various rocks and minerals which occur in Spain.

Location of sites - **Spain***

Alcántara	39.44N	6.53W	Map 23 CD 45
Alicante	38.21N	0.29W	Map 24 EF 12
Almansa	38.50N	0.55W	Map 24 EF 23
Almendralejo	38.41N	6.25W	Map 23 DE 23
Argentera, south of Quinto	41.08N	0.55E	Map 20 EF 23
Badajoz	38.53N	6.58W	Map 23 DE 34
Badalona	41.27N	2.15E	Map 20 BC 23
Barcelona	41.23N	2.11E	Map 21 CD 23
Bejar	40.23N	5.46W	Map 23 EF 56
Belchite	41.18N	0.45W	Map 23 DE 23
Brañuelas, south-east of Bembibre	42.38N	6.12W	Map 19 EF 56
Busdongo, south of Puerto de Pajares	42.59N	5.42W	Map 19 EF 45
Cadiz	36.32N	6.18W	Map 25 CD 56
Cartagena	37.36N	0.59W	Map 25 EF 34
Ciudad Real	38.59N	3.56W	Map 24 AB 23
Elche	38.16N	0.41W	Map 24 EF 12
El Ferrol	43.29N	8.14W	Map 19 BC 56

Jerez   36.41N   6.08w Map 25 CD 56

Madrid   40.24N   3.41W Map 24 BC 56
Mérida   38.55N   6.20w Map 23 DE 34

Ormaizteguí, south-   43.03N   2.15W Map 20 CD 56
west of Tolosa

Ponferrada, on road   43.22N   8.24W Map 19 BC 56
from La Coruña to
Madrid, via Lugo and
Astorga

Relleu, south-east of   38.41N   6.25w Map 23 CD 23
Badajoz

San Sadurni de Noya,   41.23N   2.11E Map 21 CD 23
Barcelona
Segovia   40.57N   4.07w Map 24 AB 56

Tarragona   41.07N   1.15E Map 21 BC 23
Tarrasa   41.34N   2.01E Map 20 CD 34

* *A.A. Continental Handbook, 1970–1*

SWEDEN

The industrial history of Sweden begins in early medieval times, with the exploitation of the copper and iron deposits and with the development of timber exports on a considerable scale. Since then, Sweden's iron and steel industries have become of world importance, and, from the nineteenth century onwards, her engineering and wood-pulp enterprises have made substantial contributions to the national prosperity, with textiles, glass, tobacco and food-processing also expanding and profitable.

Many of the earlier industrial centres were in country districts, where there was less chance of demolition, rebuilding and replanning than in urban areas. As a neutral country, Sweden was able to avoid the destruction caused by two world wars, which removed so much historically important material elsewhere. Consequently, she has an exceptional amount to offer to the visitor who is interested in the surviving evidence of yesterday's industries and transport systems. A high proportion of these old ironworks, mines, factories and canals are located in areas of great natural beauty and so there is a double pleasure to be obtained by seeking them out.

Details of only a small selection of Sweden's industrial monuments can be given here, but the list gives a good idea of the range of material that is available. It will be noticed from the sites selected, that they are all in the central and southern provinces – Daland, Värmland, Västmanland, Gästrikland, Uppland, Närke, Södermanland, Östergötland, and Småland. During the present century there has been very great investment and development in the north of the country, centred on the iron-mines, but before 1900 industry was virtually confined to Southern Sweden.

MUSEUMS

Sweden has a number of fine museums, in which the history of her industries is attractively illustrated and documented. Chief among them is the Technical Museum (Tekniska Museet, Museivägan 7) in *Stockholm*, which covers the whole field of industry. The railway Museum (Järnvägsmuseum), also in Stockholm, has a very pleasant collection of old locomotives and coaches, while a smaller collection of railway antiquities is preserved in a woodland setting at *Nässjö*, in the Hembygdspark. At *Karlskrona* there is a Naval Dockyard Museum. The famous outdoor museum at Skansen, in Stockholm, contains examples of windmills, watermills and craftsmen's workshops, brought from various parts of Sweden and re-erected in the museum-park. A section of another open-air museum, at *Ludvika*, in Dalarna, is devoted to the history of the mining industry. Both buildings and machinery have been transferred to this museum.

Several of the larger industrial concerns have their own museums. Outstanding among these are the museum of the Stora Kopparberg Company at *Falun* and of the Surahammar Bruk at *Surahammar*. The Swedish Tobacco Monopoly's museum in *Stockholm* is also worth visiting; it contains sections devoted to cultivating, processing and selling tobacco in Sweden.

TRANSPORT Canals and Bridges

Sweden has an immense number of lakes, which have for many centuries constituted an important part of the transport system. Several canal projects have provided inland water transport over long distances, by linking several lakes together.

The biggest of these canal-lake schemes is the *Göta Canal*, built between 1810 and 1832 by Baron Baltzar von Platen, with the help of Thomas Telford. It is owned by the Göta Canal Company and is now used mainly for pleasure boating.

The Göta Canal solved a serious transport problem by making it possible, in combination with the Trollhätte Canal, to cross Sweden from Stockholm to Göteborg on inland waterways. It starts from the coast of Östergötland and runs through the town of Söderköping, through the lakes Roxen and Boren to Motala, and then through Västergötland to Lake Vänern. From Vänern it is possible to continue on the Trollhätte Canal to Göteborg. The flight of locks at *Borenshult*, near Motala, in Östergötland is impressive; boats are lifted or lowered 15 metres, and the lock gates are still operated by hand.

There have been recent discussions on the possibility of widening the

Canal, in order to allow it to take the size of barge demanded by modern canal users. If this development takes place, it would necessitate the removal of all the surviving details of the nineteenth-century canal.

Another interesting canal is the *Strömsholms Canal*, linking *Smedjebacken* in Dalarna to *Mälaren* in Västmanland, which was constructed in two stages, between 1776–1792 and 1842–1860. It is no longer used for commercial purposes, but a good deal of repair work has recently been carried out, especially to the lock-gates. The canal has 31 locks, each 5.3 metres wide and of a length varying between 20.5 and 25.5 metres. The finest series of locks is at *Hallstahammar* in Västmanland.

An important and much-visited bridge is *Älvkarleby Bridge* (Carl XIII's Bridge), in Uppland. Completed in 1816, the architect was 'Captain mechanicus' Olof Forsgren, and it is the property of the State. With piers of stone and arches of timber, painted in the characteristic Swedish red, it is situated at the Älvkarleby waterfalls. The adjacent hydraulic power station was built in 1911–15.

COPPER AND SILVER MINING

The most famous mine in Sweden is the *Falun* Coppermine, in Dalarna (see plate 49). It was first worked in the eleventh century, and ore was being exported by the twelfth century. Production fell in the early sixteenth century, but new deposits were located in the 1570s and output then rose rapidly, and by 1650 the 'copper mountain' was providing most of the copper used in Europe. Copper is still mined at Falun, but with the new methods available, it is now possible to extract and market the other metals present in the ore.

Many of the old surface installations have been preserved as industrial monuments. The excellent, well-arranged Museum is housed on the site of the former administration building of the Stora Kopparberg Company, the present owners of the mine. The architect was Markscheidern Tobias Geisler and the work took fourteen years to complete, 1771–85. The Museum was established in 1922. The eighteenth-century building was then in poor condition and little of it could be preserved. However, as many of the original details as possible were incorporated in the present building, which is an exact copy of the old one, but with a new wing for displaying the Company's modern produce. The mine itself has been restored and some of the old shafts are now open to the public, who are admitted to the mine on guided tours.

The silvermine at *Sala*, in Västmanland, which is still in operation on a small scale, was first worked at the beginning of the sixteenth century. It produces lead, dolomite, silver and zinc, and was originally owned by the Crown, but the miners of Sala obtained a working lease on it in the seventeenth century. Production remained low in the seventeenth and eighteenth centuries, but rose in the nineteenth, as a result of technical improvements. There are four shafts, one of which, the Queen Christina shaft, has a timbered pavilion at the top of the shaft.

WATERWHEELS

Until the installation of steam-power, Swedish mines were drained by waterwheels and a very fine example survives at *Klockartorp* in Södermarland. This huge over-shot wheel was erected in its timbered house in 1870, and was built to drain the mines of Bredsjönäs, which were situated 1,200 metres away from the wheel itself. The water came from two lakes 1,000 metres away.

The wheel measures 13.4 metres in diameter and has 166 buckets, each capable of holding 30 litres of water. It was in use for about twenty years, before being replaced by a steam-engine. In 1968 it was completely restored and is now preserved as an industrial monument. It is Crown property.

OIL REFINING

A very early oil-refinery has been preserved in almost perfect condition near *Engelsberg*, in Central Sweden. It dates from 1876 and is a simple plant of a type common in the United States a decade or so earlier. It was built on Oljeön Island (Oil Island), near the shore of Lake Ämänningen, one of the many lakes in the Strömsholm Canal system. The stoves for heating the oil were wood-fired.

IRON WORKS

In 1927 Engelsberg oil refinery was bought by Axel Johnson, who was already the owner of the old ironworks at Engelsberg, which has been carefully preserved, complete with its blast furnace.

A number of other early blast-furnaces still exist. One is at *Åg*, in Dalarna, which was erected in 1829 and was in use until 1927. The ore was taken from the nearby mines at Vintjärn and the pig-iron was transported over the lakes to the forge at Korsån. The furnace has been carefully preserved by its owner, the Stora Kopparberg Company, and much of the original equipment, such as the wooden waterwheels, is still there.

The first furnace at *Vällorna* in Uppland was built in 1684, and the last in the 1860s. From 1774 it provided the pig-iron for Rånäs bruk. It was abandoned in the 1890s, but is still standing, though in a ruined condition.

The furnace at *Bännebol*, Uppland, situated rather remotely in the woods, made the pig-iron for Hargs bruk. The present furnace dates from 1856–57 and nearby can be seen the furnace, of about the same date, for roasting the ore. The housing for the workers and the foreman also survives.

There have been furnaces at *Motjärnshyttan*, in Värmland, since 1643. The present furnace was built in 1854, and was modernised in 1883 and again in 1901, but finally closed in 1916. The furnace has been restored and preserved by its owners, the Uddeholms Company, which has also preserved a number of other very fine furnaces in Värmland.

The iron-ore at *Dannemora* is of very high quality, and mining records go back to the fifteenth century. Pumping the water out of the mines was a serious problem. In 1726 Marten Triewald returned to Sweden, after working for some time with Thomas Newcomen, and installed a Newcomen engine at Dannemora in 1728, but it was unsuccessful. In 1735 the pumping equipment fell into the mine and in the following year the chimney was struck by lighning. The house, however, remains and it is now used as a museum.

The iron-working centre at *Björneborg*, in Värmland was established in 1656. An extensive modernisation programme was carried out in the 1870s, including the building of two new charcoal furnaces, a Bessemer foundry and a steel foundry with 14 steam-driven hammers. The Bessemer furnace was closed in 1904, and shortly afterwards a Martin furnace was brought into operation. The charcoal furnaces produced iron of a very high quality, and although they ceased working in 1954, one has been preserved by the owners, Björneborgs Jernverks.

Reference has been made earlier to 'bruks'. The bruk – the word is almost impossible to translate – is a characteristically Swedish institution. In its early form, it could best be defined as a self-contained, family-owned industrial village, dependent on water-power, with workshops, workers' houses, owner's house and all the ancillary services, such as farms, mills, shops and churches, which a self-contained community needed. Some of the bruks are architecturally very fine and worth visiting for this reason alone.

At *Brevens bruk*, Närke, the first forge was built in 1676 and the first furnace in 1733. Both were subsequently renewed, and the furnace, closed in 1932, is preserved. An engineering workshop and a foundry are still working here, producing mainly equipment for the mining, quarrying, concrete and paper industries. The property is still owned by the Gripenstedt family.

Korsån bruk, in Dalarna, was established in 1840, almost completely rebuilt in the 1860s and finally closed in 1930. The pig-iron came from Åg, 20 kilometres north of Korsån. The forge has been preserved by the owners, the Stora Kopparberg Company, and looks very much as it did in the 1860s. The walls of the forge have been taken down, but the hammers can still be seen (see plate 41) together, with the waterwheels, 7 metres in diameter, which drove them.

Forsmann bruk, in Uppland, was founded by the Crown in 1570. In 1660 it had two blast furnaces and two forges, but during the nineteenth century the furnace was situated elsewhere. In 1751 the property was bought by the firm of Finlay and Jennings, who engaged the architect Jean Eric Rehn to build a new manor, but since 1782 the bruk has belonged to the Ugglas family. Until a few years ago the bruk was complete, with the manor, workers' houses and industrial and farm buildings, but the forge and the coal-house have recently been demolished. However, the manor and the park, with its attractive little pavilions, the workers' houses and other buildings have been beautifully restored by the owners.

Another bruk founded by the Crown was *Lövsta* (1600), also in Uppland. In 1626 it was leased to the Dutchman, Willem de Besche, who took his fellow countryman Louis de Geer into partnership in 1627. In 1643 de Geer bought Lövsta, Grimo and Österby bruks in Uppland. For 300 years Lövsta was the most important of all the bruks in Uppland, and during the eighteenth century it was the most important in the whole of Sweden. Unfortunately, none of the old industrial buildings remain; the forge was pulled down in 1930, shortly after it was closed. But the setting of the bruk shows clearly how the enterprise once functioned – the manor, the workers' houses, the ponds and the beautiful park. The 1728 church is also well worth seeing, with its famous organ by Johan Niklas Cahman.

In the sixteenth century there were two blast furnaces at *Österby bruk,* in Uppland, with two large and six smaller hammers, and by the seventeenth century there were as many as five furnaces. The bruk was owned by the Crown to begin with, but in 1643 it was acquired by Louis de Geer, and in the eighteenth century it was owned by the families Grill and Tamm. The eighteenth-century forge has been preserved as an industrial monument, and its machinery is still there – the waterwheel, the hammers, and the hand-tools used by the smiths.

Munkfors bruk, Värmland, is of great importance in the history of technology. The bruk, on the river Klarälven, was founded in 1670. In 1864–67 the manager, J. F. Lundin, experimented with a method of smelting scrap iron with pig-iron, a method similar to that developed by Siemens-Martin and patented by them. The first Martin furnace at Munkfors was installed in 1868. In 1887 pioneering experiments with cold-rolled steel were carried out successfully at Munkfors and the first buildings for this process were erected on the island of Laxholmen in the river Klarälven. These buildings are still in use.

Another pioneering iron-making centre was *Edsken bruk* in Gästrikland. The Bessemer process was introduced to Sweden in 1857: the equipment was made by V. and J. Galloway of Manchester and shipped to Gävle, and from July 1858, Bessemer steel was in regular production at Edsken. In October 1858 Bessemer's own company in Sheffield bought 100 tons of pig-iron from Edsken. The original blast furnace and Bessemer converters have been restored by the Company, Sandvikens Jernverks, and preserved as an industrial monument.

Sandviken, in Gästrikland, was laid out as a large ironworks in 1862, shortly after the Bessemer process had turned out to be successful. G. F. Göransson was the first person to use Henry Bessemer's method in Sweden and it was Göransson who founded Sandviken. Twelve steam-hammers were installed in the forge and one of them has been kept as an industrial monument, outside the office building. One of the Bessemer converters can also be seen in the park surrounding the works.

Another post-Bessemer ironworks was *Hagfors*, in Värmland. Hagfors came into being in the 1870s, shortly after the introduction of the Bessemer process. After the coming of the railways in Sweden, the Uddeholms Company decided to concentrate the production of iron at a number of smaller bruks into one large works. A new site, at Hagfors, was chosen for the purpose, and the first furnace started producing iron in 1878. The ironworks have expanded ever since, as the older buildings have been replaced, but the Bessemer furnace is still standing intact, with its two converters, although it is no longer used. The converters are within the industrial area and cannot be visited without special permission.

Any list of historic Swedish ironworks must include *Surahammar*, in Västmanland. There is evidence of a hammer mill here since the first half of the seventeenth century, and there was probably one long before that. The works remained small until the 1840s, when two puddling furnaces and a rolling mill were built. During the nineteenth century Surahammar became well known for the manufacture of railway material, especially wheels and axles. Since then it has made forgings, castings and heavy plates for the electrical industry. The old forge is still used as a museum, and is one of the best company museums in Sweden.

HARBOURS

The bruks in Uppland had their own harbours where the bar-iron was stored before being exported. *Ängskär* was the harbour for Lövsta. The early eighteenth-century warehouses were small and built of wood, but the coast of Uppland was heavily damaged by the Russians in 1719–21 and the two remaining warehouses, Ängskär and Hargshamn, were solidly built of stone. Ängskär dates from 1758, and although preserved, is not at present in use for any purpose. It contains a number of separate storerooms.

The stone warehouse at *Hargshamn*, with iron shutters painted black, was built, probably for Hargsbruk, in the 1750s (see plate 43). Bar-iron was kept here during the winter months, until the coast was clear of ice and ships were able to anchor safely in the harbour.

TEXTILES

Survivals of the Swedish textile industry are not extensive. One interesting example is at *Strömsbro*, near Gävle, Gästrikland. In 1849 it was decided to build a new cotton mill, for both spinning and weaving, on the Testebo river. The design of the building and the supply of equipment were entrusted to English firms; and the 150-hp waterwheel, 12.2 metres in diameter, was made by Fairbairns, of Manchester. The cotton mills are now closed and the machinery has gone, and at present a brewery is using the building as a store.

Norrköping, in Östergötland, was the centre of the woollen industry which developed in Sweden during the seventeenth and eighteenth centuries. During the 1840s and 1850s a number of new companies were formed in Norrköping, with capital to build on a larger scale than previously and to buy new machinery from England. Both cotton and woollen mills were built along the Motala river, mostly using waterpower.

During the past twenty years, changes in the structure of the textile industry have caused many of the old firms to close down, and there is now no cotton mill on the Motala still working. Some of the buildings are derelict and due for demolition; others are being used as stores. Most of the riverside property has been bought by Holmens Bruks AB, which controls the local woollen and paper industries.

PAPER

The old papermill at *Ösjöfors*, in Östergötland is owned by the Technical Museum in Stockholm and is preserved as an industrial monument. It was established in 1777, to make paper from cotton and linen rags, and production continued as late as 1926, when it was one of the last paper mills in Sweden worked by hand-labour.

Paper-making on a very different scale was carried on at *Edsvalla bruk*, in Värmland. Edsvalla has had an interesting history. It was originally an iron-making bruk, but changed to timber production in the late nineteenth century. In 1907–8 it was converted into a pulp-mill, using the sulphite process and for many years produced 35,000 tons of pulp a year. In 1960 a new and impressive boiler house was erected, but the mill was closed in 1967 and is now empty.

SHIPBUILDING

Shipbuilding is one of Sweden's traditional industries, and two of its monuments are particularly outstanding. *Karlskrona*, in Belkinge, was established in the seventeenth century as the main port for the Swedish Navy, and the harbour and its fortifications were constructed from the 1680s onwards. The Vasaskjulet building was completed in 1767 to house small galleys while they were being repaired. It is an impressive building, with its wide-span wooden roof, painted red.

The shipbuilding yard and workshop at *Motala* (see plate 11) is the oldest in Sweden, and its history is linked with that of the Göta Canal. It was established in 1822 by Baltzar von Platen and the first manager was a Scotsman, Daniel Fraser, who began shipbuilding there. He was followed by Edvard Carlsund, who introduced the propeller in Sweden. The first paddle-steamer, of wood, was built at Motala in 1831, the first iron ship in 1842, the first propeller-driven ship in 1844 and the first locomotive in 1861.

GLASS AND FURNITURE

The newer Swedish industries have also made their mark on the landscape, and some of them have now acquired a considerable history. Swedish glass has a world-wide reputation. The industry is centred on Småland and there are 35 glassworks around *Växjö* and *Nybro*. The glass-works at *Orrefors* and *Kosta* are open to the public (except during the month of July). Småland's glass museum is at *Växjö*.

Småland is also an important centre of the furniture industry, the principal towns involved being *Almhult*, *Badafors* and *Velland*.

WINDMILLS

Windmills have never been such a characteristic feature of the Swedish landscape as they have of the Dutch. Given such an abundance of water power, the Swedes very reasonably built watermills rather than windmills. One very famous windmill, however, is in *Stockholm* itself, at Waldemar-sudde. This is an oil-seed mill, dating back to 1784, and it was built on the same principles as contemporary oil-mills in the Netherlands (see plate 33). It has been restored twice, once in 1900 by Prince Eugen, who lived at Waldermarsudde, and a second time, more thoroughly in 1960, and is now a magnificent example of the millwright's skill, with its complex system of massive wooden machinery in excellent condition. Prince Eugen's house is now an art museum.

Location of sites - **Sweden***

Åg, north-west of Falun   60.47N 16.02E Map 6 DE 56
Almhult   56.32N 14.10E Map 8 BC 34
Älvkarleby   60.35N 17.30E Map 6 EF 56
Ängskär, north-east of   59.44N 18.48E Map 6 FG 45
  Norrtälje

Badafors, south-west   56.44N 15.48E Map 8 CD 34
  of Almhult
Bännebol, north-east of   59.49N 16.47E Map 6 EF 45
  Heby
Björneborg, south-east   59.14N 14.15E Map 6 CD 23
  of Kristinehamn
Borenshult, near   see reference below for Motala
  Motala
Brevens bruk, south-   59.01N 15.35E Map 6 DE 23
  east of Orebro

Dannemora, north-east   60.13N 17.50E Map 6 EF 45
  of Österby bruk

Edsken bruk, south-east   60.38N 17.20E Map 6 EF 56
  of Gävle
Edsvalla bruk, north-   59.26N 13.13E Map 6 BC 34
  east of Högboda
Engelsberg, north-east   59.58N 16.01E Map 6 DE 45
  of Sala

Falun   60.37N 15.40E Map 6 DE 56
Forsmann bruk, north-   60.20N 16.25W Map 6 DE 45
  east of Avesla

Göta Canal   From 58.50N 15.00E Map 6 CD 12

Hagfors   60.03N 13.45E Map 6 BC 45
Hallstahammar, west of   59.26N 16.17E Map 6 DE 34
  Västeras
Hargshamn, south of   60.09N 18.28E Map 6 FG 45
  Grisslehamn

Karlskrona, Belkinge   56.10N 15.35E Map 8 CD 23
Klockartorp, east of   58.59N 14.35E Map 6 CD 23
  Askersund
Korsån bruk, north-   60.38N 16.20E Map 6 DE 56
  east of Falun
Kosta, north of Orrefors   56.50N 15.25E Map 8 CD 34

Lövsta, north of Heby	58.58N	17.34E	Map	6 EF 45
Ludvika	60.08N	15.14E	Map	6 CD 45
Motala	58.34N	15.05E	Map	6 CD 12
Motjärnshyttan, north-east of Munkfors	59.56N	13.59E	Map	6 BC 34
Munkfors bruk	59.50N	13.35E	Map	6 BC 34
Nässjö	57.39N	14.40E	Map	8 BC 45
Norrköping	58.35N	16.10E	Map	6 DE 12
Nybro	56.44N	15.55E	Map	8 DE 34
Orrefors	56.48N	15.45E	Map	8 CD 34
Ösjöfors, south-east of Linköping	58.10N	15.45E	Map	6 DE 12
Österby bruk	60.13N	17.55E	Map	6 EF 45
Sala	59.55N	16.38E	Map	6 DE 45
Sandviken	60.38N	16.50E	Map	6 DE 56
Stockholm	59.20N	18.95E	Map	6 FG 34
Strömsbro, north-west of Gävle	60.42N	17.09E	Map	6 EF 56
Strömsholms Canal (Smedjebacken-Mälaren)	60.08N	15.25E	Map	6 DE 45
Surahammar, north-west of Västeras	59.42N	16.14E	Map	6 DE 34
Vällorna, north-east of Uppsala	59.58N	18.20E	Map	6 FG 56
Velland, south of Almhult	56.43N	15.47E	Map	8 CD 34
Växjö	56.52N	14.50E	Map	8 CD 34

* *A.A. Continental Handbook, 1970–1*

57 Cloth-drying tower, St Gallen, Switzerland. Second half of the eighteenth century. The tower was probably used for drying cotton-cloth, after dyeing. Switzerland established a cotton industry surprisingly early. (*see page* 153)

58 Watertower, near Dunkirk, France. *c.* 1910. A well-preserved example of early twentieth-century concrete construction, illustrating French proficiency in the material at a relatively early date for a structure of this size.

59 Cooling tower, near Mons, Belgium. *c.* 1920. Constructed of prefabricated concrete sections.

60 Gasholder, Düsseldorf, West Germany. *c.* 1910. A very light, graceful structure, which fortunately survived the war-time bombing of this highly industrialised part of Germany.

61 Gasholder, Finchley, London, England. *c.* 1890. An exceptionally graceful example of a type widely built in Britain during the latter part of the nineteenth century.

62 Pottery kilns, Stoke-on-Trent, England. The four patterns of kiln shown in the photograph date from 1830 to 1900. The landscape around Stoke contained hundreds of these kilns only 25 years ago, but very few are now left.

63 Garage, rue de Ponthieu, Paris, France. 1920. A particularly interesting and well-designed early reinforced concrete structure by Auguste Perret, one of the leading French architects of the present century. (*see page* 70)

64 Brede Værk, Lyngby, Denmark. 1908. An early Danish example of reinforced
concrete factory construction. Denmark was one of the pioneering countries in
concrete technology. (*see page* 51)

65 Bodega, Jerez, Spain. *c.* 1800. This is the traditional type of sherry bodega. The more recent examples have a more factory-like appearance. (*see page* 134)

66 Capstan wine-press, Epernay, France. Seventeenth century. One of the collection of early wine-presses preserved in the Champagne Mercier Museum.

67 Wine factory, Brile, Yugoslavia. 1955. The modern type, with a large annual production and serving a considerable area of vineyards.

68 Wine-processing building, near Brile, Yugoslavia. Probably *c.* 1850. This type of building, containing the wine-press, is still found throughout the wine-growing districts of Yugoslavia, although very few such presses are still operational.

69 Milk-pressing factory, Ølgod, West Jutland, Denmark. 1882. Denmark's first commercial milk-factory. Restored in 1950, using the original machinery. (*see page* 54)

70 Plaque commemorating the handing over of the Bor Copperworks, Yugoslavia,
to workers' control. 1953. This plaque is typical of many erected in Yugoslavia
during the 1950s. Transfer was not automatic, it had to be earned by proving
efficiency.

71 Obukhova steel foundry, near Leningrad, U.S.S.R. Photograph taken in 1900. An example of nineteenth-century factory building, very similar to many factories in Western Europe.

72 Gubner textile mills, Moscow, U.S.S.R. Photograph taken in 1887. The mills still exist, but they have been much modified and extended.

SWITZERLAND

Industrial development began late in Switzerland. It started with textiles and gradually extended to general engineering. The Federation has no coal, practically no iron and very little in the way of other mineral deposits. Its industries are almost wholly dependent on imported raw materials and its exports are mostly high in value and small in bulk; watches, shoes and scientific instruments are typical Swiss products, although a substantial heavy engineering and machine-building trade has been developed during the present century. The industry which brings Switzerland the highest proportion of its income and much of its international prestige – its banking and financial services – has no monuments, and the other very big source of income, tourism, has very few.

MUSEUMS

When it is completed the National Technical Museum, known as Technorama, will be one of the finest in the world. It has been deliberately sited in the engineering town of *Winterthur* (Pflanzschulstrasse 30), rather than in one of the more glamorous cities, like Zürich or Geneva, to emphasise its practical importance. Switzerland's prosperity depends on its technical skill and inventiveness, and in recent years too many of its best brains and ex-apprentices have been leaving for America and Australia. The purpose of Technorama is therefore to stimulate the imagination of the country's young people, to make them proud of Switzerland's technological past and to reassure them that Switzerland has a technological future.

A Guide to the Industrial Archaeology of Europe

The tradition of private enterprise is extremely strong in Swiss industry. Technorama owes its existence as much to the initiative of individual firms, especially Sulzer, as to the Government. A very careful watch is kept on public spending, and where historic monuments are concerned the first criterion is probably that the money spent on restoration and preservation shall help the tourist industry, and the second that it shall be of educational value. Technorama is the product of worried economists and politicians rather more than of educational pioneers. Switzerland is not big enough or rich enough to indulge in luxuries; despite its surface gloss and opulence, most of its citizens need to watch their expenditure very carefully and are accustomed to ask for good value in exchange for their taxes.

All the major cities and many of the smaller ones have excellent historical museums. *Basel* has a museum entirely devoted to transport on the Rhine, 'Our Way to the Sea'. Its official title is the somewhat forbidding Rheinschiffahrtausstellung and it is located on the Rhine Harbour, at *Basel-Kleinhüningen*. The Postal and Telecommunications Museum (Schweizerisches P.T.T. Museum, Helvetia Platz 4) is in *Bern*, and there is a Science Museum (Musée d'histoire des sciences, 128 rue de Lausanne) in *Geneva*.

The watch and clock industry is well documented in the Musée d'horlogerie at *La Chaux-de-Fonds*. The Rolex Company was established in *Geneva* as Montres Rolex, Geneva, in 1919. The factory is entirely modern, but includes a valuable collection of antique watches and historic Rolex pieces – the first fully waterproof watch, the first reliable self-winding watch, and the first watch to show the date. There are other horological museums at Geneva, and *Le Locle*, and at *Fontainemelon*, at the Fabrique d'horlogerie de Fontainemelon. At *St Gallen* there is a Museum of Industrial and Applied Art (Industrie- und Gewerbemuseum, Vadianstrasse 2), which has a good lace and embroidery section. The Swiss Transport Museum is at *Lucerne* (Lidostrasse 5), and is aimed unashamedly at the tourist – the guide describes it as 'the most modern and comprehensive of its kind in Europe'. There are restaurants in Switzerland's 'oldest lake steamer and earliest dining-car'; the 'oldest lake-steamer', the *Rigi*, is now safely on dry land, in the Museum Courtyard. It was built, somewhat surprisingly, in London in 1847, and spent 105 years steaming up and down the Vierwaldstättersee. The Museum is a lively place, which makes good use of working models and is excellently placed, between the lake and the railway main line, to attract visitors. The guide is printed in twelve languages, including Japanese.

The Bally Museum at Felgarten, *Schönenwerd* is the finest shoe-museum in Europe, if not in the world. The Bally concern began making shoes at Schönenwerd in 1851. Felgarten was for many years the management centre of the firm. The museum now installed there includes the office occupied by the founder of the firm, Carl Franz Bally, and an old shoemaker's workshop. There is also a magnificent and beautifully arranged collection showing the history of shoes throughout the world and of those made by Bally during the past hundred years.

TRANSPORT Railways

Railways, like industry, came relatively late to Switzerland, and there is little surviving material of any historic interest before the 1860s. The line from Strasbourg reached Basel in 1844, but the first railway to be constructed within Switzerland itself ran from Zürich to Baden. The *St Gotthard Tunnel* (at Goschener) opened in 1894, provided the first through service from Switzerland to Italy and this, like the *Simplon Tunnel* (1906), the longest tunnel in the world, is a monument to both Swiss and Italian civil engineering.

Switzerland can also claim another first in the field of railways, the *Vitznau-Rigi* railway (1871), which was the first rack-railway in Europe and provided technical experience for many similar railways, in Switzerland and elsewhere. A locomotive used on this railway is preserved in the Transport Museum; it was the first to be built at the famous locomotive works in *Winterthur* and bears the proud number Fabrik-Nr.1, and entered service in 1873. The Museum also has a steam-driven coach from the Pilatus railway (1900), the steepest rack-railway in the world.

The railway stations at *Lucerne* (1882) and *Basel* (1882) have been little altered and are good examples of the monumental style current throughout Western Europe in the last quarter of the nineteenth century. The power-station at *Amsteg*, which supplies electricity to the railway, dates from 1903 and was built soon after the Federal Railways (SBB) assumed responsibility for the railways in Switzerland.

Swiss railways were difficult and expensive to build. They demanded a great many tunnels and bridges, as any railway journey through Switzerland reveals. One of the more remarkable viaducts is at *Langwies*, on the Chur-Arosa line. 187 metres long and 62 metres high, with a main span of 96 metres, it was the first reinforced concrete structure in Switzerland (1870). With Switzerland's abundant water-power and non-existent coal resources, electrification of the railways was the obvious solution. The first line to be electrified (1888) was Vevey-Montreux-Chillon, a narrow-gauge line and the first main-line stretch was Burgdorf–Thun, the pioneering piece of main-line electrification in Europe.

TRANSPORT   Bridges

There are many fine wooden bridges in Switzerland, and one of the best is the road-bridge over the River Urnausch, at *St Gallen*, preserved as a national monument. It was built to take traffic from St Gallen to Herisau, but is now used only by pedestrians. Dating from 1780, it was designed and built by Hans Ulrich Grubermann, who was famous for his large timber constructions, in both churches and secular buildings. His bridge at St Gallen has a span of 30 metres and is in excellent condition. One of the finest of Grubermann's church roofs is in the Protestant Church at *Wädenswil*, in Canton Zürich; it is earlier than the St Gallen bridge (1764–67), but shows the same mastery of large timbers. Other famous bridges built by Hans Ulrich Grubermann include the two-span (58.7 metres and 54.8 metres) covered timber bridge over the Rhine and Schaffhausen.

Another bridge can be seen at *Spisegg* near St Gallen. It is on the St Gallen–Gaiserwald road spanning the river Sitter, and was built by Johann Ulrich Schefer in 1782. In the 1920s the roof on the southern side of the bridge was removed, in order to provide more light for people walking across. In 1961 it was fully restored and it is now classified and preserved as a national monument.

The Swiss wooden bridges, like Alpine gabled houses, have great tourist value and are understandably much photographed. Their picturesque appearance should not, however, prevent us from appreciating the great skill which went into their construction, and they should be seen as important examples of timber technology. The bridges at *Lucerne* illustrate almost the whole of the history of bridge-building in Switzerland. The Kapellbrücke (1333) (see plate 5) and the Spreuerbrücke (1408) are both covered wooden bridges. The Reussbrücke (1852) is the oldest of Lucerne's iron bridges, which replaced an earlier wooden bridge. Towards the end of the nineteenth century several new bridges were built over the Reuss, including the graceful pedestrian bridge, from the Theatre to the Old Town Hall, the Geissmatt Bridge and the St Karli Bridge, all of which are iron bridges. There are two nineteenth-century railway bridges crossing the Reuss, one carrying the Gotthard line and the other the Zürich line. The Seebrücke (1936), a steel and concrete bridge, carries most of the traffic between the two parts of the city.

BREWING

One of the largest breweries in Switzerland is the Brauerei Haldengut at *Winterthur* which was founded in 1800. The earliest surviving building dates from 1842, although it is no longer used for brewing purposes, and it is now entirely surrounded by more recent buildings.

IRON WORKS

There are a number of survivals of small-scale ironworks, which used charcoal as a fuel. These include eighteenth-century hammer-forges at *Worblaufen*, near Bern and at *Mühlehorn*, in Canton Glarus. The site of the old iron-mines on the *Gontzen* is still visible at *Sargans*.

SALT MINING

The fifteenth-century salt-mines at *Bex* are still in operation, although considerably modernised, and can be visited. They belong to the Canton of Vaud and are worked on behalf of the Canton by the Société Vaudoise des Mines et Salines de Bex.

TEXTILES

With an abundance of timber easily available, Switzerland has always specialised in wooden structures for a wide range of purposes. One very curious example of a timber building is the drying tower at *St Gallen* where linen cloth was produced as early as the twelfth century. Until the eighteenth century the newly-woven lengths of cloth were spread or hung out in the open air, both for bleaching and for drying after the cloth had been dyed. In the middle of the eighteenth century, the district added cotton-manufacturing to its occupations. The drying tower at St Gallen, which is no longer in use, appears to date from the second half of the eighteenth century, and was probably used to dry dyed cotton-cloth, not linen (see plate 58).

In Switzerland, more than in any other European country, with the possible exception of Holland, continuous modernisation is essential for economic survival. For this reason, and because in a small country space is always in short supply, old industrial plant is quickly scrapped, or sent to a museum, and old industrial buildings are rebuilt or transformed to meet new conditions. Except in the rural areas and on the railways, Switzerland cannot be described as a paradise for the industrial archeologist although, with its excellent museums and libraries, it is a very good place for the industrial historian.

Location of sites - **Switzerland***

Amsteg	46.47N	8.41E	Map 18 AG 56
Basel	47.33N	7.36E	Map 14 CD 12
Bex	46.16N	7.01E	Map 17 EF 45
Fontainemelon, near Le Locle	47.04N	6.45E	Map 14 BC 12
Geneva	46.13N	6.09E	Map 17 DE 45
Gontzen, north of Sargans	47.03N	9.25E	Map 14 DE 12
La Chaux-de-Fonds	47.04N	6.45E	Map 14 BC 12
Langwies, west-south-west of Davos	46.50N	9.44E	Map 18 BC 56
Le Locle	47.04N	6.45E	Map 14 BC 12
Lucerne	47.03N	8.17E	Map 14 CD 12
Mühlehorn, north-east of Nafels	47.08N	9.11E	Map 14 DE 12
Sargans	47.03N	9.27E	Map 14 DE 12
Schönenwerd, south-east of Aarau	47.23N	8.01E	Map 14 CD 12
Simplon Tunnel (Brig)	46.19N	8.00E	Map 17 FG 45
Spisegg, north-west of St Gallen	47.15N	8.40E	Map 14 DE 12
St Gallen	47.25N	9.23E	Map 14 DE 12
St Gotthard Tunnel (Göschener)	46.40N	8.36E	Map 17 FG 56
Vitznau	47.01N	8.30E	Map 17 FG 56
Wädenswil	47.14N	8.41E	Map 14 DE 12
Winterthur	47.30N	8.45E	Map 14 DE 12
Worblaufen, north-east of Bern	46.57N	7.26E	Map 17 EF 56

* *A.A. Continental Handbook, 1970–1*

U.S.S.R.

Until the Revolution there were only two industrial regions in Russia of any consequence, one centred on Moscow and the other on St Petersburg. The development of St Petersburg as an industrial city with a major ship-building yard was largely the work of Peter the Great. The eighteenth-century foundries and forges there used some iron from Sweden and Finland and from the Tula region of Russia but even more from the Urals. This was, of course, charcoal-iron. The industrial development of the Urals, too, was begun by Peter the Great, who established copper and iron smelters and arms factories in the area. Yekaterinberg (Sverdlodsk) was founded in 1723 and Yegoshika (Perm) in 1922. Charcoal-smelting in Russia continued well into the nineteenth century, much later than else-where in Europe, but in the second half of the century Donets Coke and Krivoi Rog iron-ore supplanted the charcoal-smelted iron and changed the scale of the industry.

It is not generally realised that in 1725 Russia led the world in the production of iron, with a total output of 150,000 tons, a figure not reached in Britain until the end of the century.

Because of the Czar's military needs, the mining of iron-ore had in-creased since 1600 more than that of any other mineral. This increase came wholly from the Urals, where there was not only a higher grade of ore than in Central Russia, but vast regions of forest for charcoal-making.

By the end of Peter the Great's reign the number of factories in Russia had risen from about a dozen to something like 200. Some of them – iron-works, armament works and textile mills – employed 500–1000 people. At the beginning of the nineteenth century, except in metallurgy and one or two new industries, such as cotton, urban artisans and rural cottage manu-facturers were responsible together for a greater volume of production

155

than factory industry. The first spinning machines were introduced into Russia in 1793 at the State cotton factory at Schlüsselburg. The first steam engine to be used in the cotton industry began operating in St Petersburg in 1805.

Capitalist-type industry, using steam-power and machinery, did not really begin in Russia until the 1840s. It was greatly helped by the repeal, in 1842, of British legislation forbidding the export of machinery. By 1862, 103 of the 374 larger factories in the St Petersburg province were using steam power. Even in that year, however, heavy industry was of relatively small importance. In terms of people employed, iron foundries took fifth place in St Petersburg and eleventh in Moscow.

By 1914 much development had taken place in Russian industry, but production was still much behind that of the U.S.A., Britain, Germany, France and even Belgium. In that year, Russia stood fifth among world-producers of coal and steel. Most of the coal came from the Donets, which had a very high ratio of labour to output, compared with other parts of Europe, and most of the iron from the Ukraine. Most of Russia's petroleum came from Baku, where, within 16 kilometres of the city, there were 100 companies operating 736 wells and where the oil was transported to the Black Sea coast both by pipeline and by camel.

It was to a great extent foreigners, not Russians, who were responsible for the country's pre-Revolution industrial growth. In 1916, the proportion of foreign capital employed in the principal industries was: mining, 91 per cent.; metallurgy, 42 per cent.; textiles, 28 per cent.; chemicals, 50 per cent. Russia's capitalists were interested mainly in textiles, and especially cotton. In 1916, textiles were the leading Russian industry, with about a third of the total value of all industrial production. It was fourth in world order, a wholly modern factory-industry protected by high tariffs.

By 1928, when the First Five Year Plan started, most of Russian industry was in an obsolescent, run-down condition. The extensive modernisation which took place from then onwards, especially in the coal and iron and steel industries, caused much of the old plant to fall out of use. This fact, together with huge war-time destruction in the Western parts of the country, means that most of Russia's industry today is carried on in buildings and on sites which are no earlier than the 1930s.

Industrial monuments dating from the eighteenth and nineteenth centuries are consequently few, and a high proportion of the buildings put up during the present century were destroyed or severely damaged during the war with Germany, between 1939-45. It is hardly surprising, therefore, that the Russian, and indeed the East European, definition of a technological or industrial musem is rather different from what is generally understood elsewhere in Europe. Russian museums of this kind make heavy use of models and photographs, and display a great deal of modern material. They tend to be exhibitions quite as much as museums, with past and present flowing into one another. The tourist has to adjust his thinking in other directions too, since travel for non-Russians is fairly strictly confined to certain prescribed routes, although within the area that can normally be visited there are a number of interesting industrial monuments which have somehow survived the battles and the modernisation fever of the past fifty years.

MUSEUMS

Leningrad has several museums which are linked to research or professional institutes. The Transport Engineers Institute, at 50 Sadovaya Street, contains a very good transport museum, founded in 1830, which is the only such museum in the Soviet Union. Models form a considerable proportion of the exhibition. The Institute of Mines, at 4 University Quay, is installed, like the Transport Museum, in an elegant early nineteenth-century building on the model of the Temple of Poseidon at Paestum. It is primarily a geological museum, but has a model mine with galleries of more than 210 metres to illustrate mining techniques. The Museum and Institute for Ceramic Research is linked to the famous Lomonosov porcelain factory (next to the Babushkin Park). Established in 1749, the factory originally produced entirely for the Court, but nowadays it makes electrical and scientific glass and porcelain in addition to the traditional art ceramics. Since 1918 it has been directed by the Organisation for the Extension of Popular Culture. Also in Leningrad, at Soyuza Sviazi 7, is the A. S. Popov Central Museum of Communications.

In recent years the Soviet Union has set up a number of regional open-air museums. Details of three of them are given here, as indications of the policy which is being followed and of the scale of the planning. The Kolomenakoje Open-air Museum, an extra-mural branch of the Moscow Historical Museum, is on the south side of *Moscow*, on the Moskva river. The core of the museum is a church and group of village buildings which are on their original site and are well preserved. Buildings from other areas have been added from time to time, although not in any markedly methodical fashion. Among the new arrivals is a 'meadery' (medovaraja), a small plant for making mead, brought from the village of Preobrazenskoje, near Moscow, where it had been in operation since the middle of the seventeenth century. Kolomenakoje would seem well suited to extensive development as a major outdoor museum of industry and technology.

The museum at *Kize* in Karelia is bigger and better organised. It is in pleasant countryside and aims to provide a good selection of vernacular buildings from the province, and among the exhibits is a combined wind and watermill (1875), entirely constructed of wood, from Berezovajeselga.

The third museum is in the Esthonian State Park and was established in 1958. It contains a 250-year-old smithy from Kahala, in the north of Esthonia, a watermill from the same village and two windmills, one from the island of Vormsi and the other from Nätsi.

A new museum, at *Tallin*, on the Baltic, puts special emphasis on old workshops and on buildings – such as net-stores – belonging to the fishing industry. The Karelian State Museum of Regional History in *Petrozavodsk* (Zavodskaya pl. 1) includes an open-air museum.

TRANSPORT   Canals

Transport is a traditional problem in Russia. Russian roads were notoriously bad in the eighteenth and nineteenth centuries and even as late as 1964 there were only 360,000 kilometres of surfaced road in the whole of the Soviet Union, of which no more than 118,400 kilometres had an asphalt or concrete surface.

Because of the poor roads, Russia has always put great emphasis on its rivers and canals. The Volga is the lynch-pin of the waterway system. If one includes its tributaries and canals and canalised rivers, the Volga provides 114,000 kilometres of navigable waterways. The main nineteenth-century improvements were the canal built by Nicholas II to link the Ob and the Yenisey and the Volga–Baltic link, which extended from *Leningrad* to *Rybinsk*. Of the total of 1,112 kilometres, 309 are canals. There are 38 locks and the summit of the canal is 121 metres above sea-level.

From the 1930s onwards, the canal system has been continuously improved. In the 1930s the work was done by convict labour. Two large projects carried out in this way were the Moscow–Volga canal (1937) and the completion of the Baltic–White Sea canal (1933). This 232 kilometres gave a direct water link from Leningrad to *Belomorsk*.

TRANSPORT   Railways

Railway development in Russia was slow. The first public railway (1837) ran from Petersburg to the Imperial Palace, Tsarskoye Selo, 22 kilometres away. The station at *Tsarskoye Selo* is now known as Pushkin Station and trains run to it from the Vitebsk station in Leningrad. In the walling of the Warsaw Station, also in *Leningrad*, is a large panel showing the first train to run from there and the original station building. Railway stations were inevitable casualties in the 1939–45 war and most of those in towns and cities between Moscow and the Western borders of the U.S.S.R. were either destroyed or severely damaged. The first railway line of any consequence in Russia was from Leningrad to Moscow (1851), and the great West-East railway, the Trans-Siberian, was built in stages between 1892 and 1904. The character of the Russian landscape presented the country's railway-builders with problems different from those which had to be faced in other European countries. Very little was required in the way of tunnels, cuttings, viaducts and major embankments, so these typical items of railway engineering were not of great importance. Large numbers of rivers and streams had to be bridged and track laid over boggy land and shifting sand. In many places, the main task of the Russian railway engineer has been to get a sufficiently solid and reliable trackbed and to discover enough ballast without needing to go prodigious distances for it. Railway mileage doubled between 1913 and 1941. The great achievement of the First Five Year Plan (1928–32) was the Turksib railway, a 1,440-kilometre line linking Central Asia and Western Siberia. The coal-mining town of Karaganda and the metallurgical centre of Magnitogorsk were connected to the Turksib by new lines.

FACTORIES IN AND AROUND LENINGRAD

One of the oldest factories in Leningrad, and certainly the most famous, is the Kirov tractor works. It was established as an engineering works in 1801 and was bought by the engineer, Putilov, in 1868. Putilov enlarged it and until the Revolution of 1917 the works was called by his name. The strike at the Putilov works sparked off the Revolution of 1905. Another revolutionary monument in Leningrad, the Finland Station, where Lenin arrived from Switzerland in 1917, in a sealed train, was demolished and rebuilt in 1960. The Red October (Krasny Oktyabr) power station helps to redress the balance. In capitalist times it was known as the Utkina Zavod power station; it was begun in 1913, but war and revolution prevented its completion until 1921.

Among the earlier monuments are the Tuchkov-Bruian warehouses, also known as Biron Castle, in Leo Tolstoy Square, built by Rinaldi in 1763; and 21 Sadovaya Street, which was the headquarters of the National Bank under the old régime and now houses the State Bank for the North West (Gosbank) and the regional financial administration. It was built by Zuarenghi in 1783–8.

On the Moscow Prospekt can be seen the old city slaughter house, an impressive early nineteenth-century building, with three fine porches each with a bronze ox-head in the centre. At *Sestroretsk*, 53 kilometres from Leningrad on the confluence of the Sestra and Chernaya rivers is an arms factory founded by Peter I in 1714. Throughout the eighteenth and nineteenth centuries it was one of the most important in Russia; after the Revolution, however, it was converted to the production of measuring instruments and now specialises in cutting tools.

The city of Leningrad is linked to the naval base and docks at *Kronstadt* by the Moskoi Canal, which is 27.4 metres long and was completed in 1900. Kronstadt itself, however, does not welcome foreign visitors.

FACTORIES IN AND AROUND MOSCOW

The Moscow industrial complex is extensive, but most of the buildings belong to the period since 1930. Motorists are not allowed to travel more than 25 miles from the Kremlin without special permission, so that an extensive tour of the largest and most varied of the Soviet Union's industrial areas is not possible without much trouble and considerable luck. Certain industrial monuments can, however, be easily discovered and visited. Several of these are on the Moskva-Sophiskaya Quay. In the seventeenth and eighteenth centuries there were many large water-powered mills along this quay. At No. 4 one can see parts of the four buildings which comprised the first textile factory in Moscow (c. 1720). The former Gustav Liszt machine tool factory, renamed the Red Torch factory after the Revolution, is at No. 12.

South of the Kremlin, on the Bersenevskaya canal embankment, is the Krasny Oktyabr confectionery factory. This was the old Einem factory of Tsarist days and its products are still famous. Also in Moscow itself is the Arsenal, a long, classical building dominating Manezhnaya Square, which was built for Peter the Great by the German architect, Christopher Konrad, and was restored on 1922. Before the Revolution of 1917 most of the war material controlled by the Moscow region was stocked here.

Outside Moscow, at *Izmailovo*, on the road to Vladimir, a number of large and important factories grew up during the nineteenth century. They included the enterprises controlled by Goujon, Danhauer and Kayser, all subsequently renamed and enlarged. The old Goujon engineering works is now the Hammer and Sickle factory and makes tractors.

FACTORIES IN KIEV AND TULA

Kiev was an industrial centre of some importance towards the end of the Tsarist period. Among the factories to be built there in the later nineteenth century were the Greter and Krivanck agricultural machinery factory, in the Shuliava suburb; the South Russia mechanical engineering works, and the Central Railway Workshops for South Russia. These factories are still there, in the sense that production continues on the same sites, but Kiev was occupied by the Germans between 1941 and 1943 and there was enormous destruction, both at the time of its capture and recapture.

Other nineteenth-century factories are to be found, mostly greatly modified and enlarged, at *Tula*. In the nineteenth century Tula was a kind of Russian Sheffield, specialising in armaments, accordions and samovars. Today's factories are concerned especially with the more expensive type of consumer goods, such as washing machines and bicycles. The U.S.S.R. has a well-organised system for restoring and preserving national monuments, but those selected for such treatment are nearly all of the kind which are valued by art historians – cathedrals, churches, palaces and public buildings of great architectural merit. The policy towards industrial monuments is quite different from that which operates in East Germany, partly because there are far fewer industrial monuments to preserve, partly because it has been considered essential to emphasise the length of the Russian cultural tradition, and partly because it is felt, probably correctly, that the workers need palaces as an antidote to factories.

Location of sites - U.S.S.R.*

Belomorsk	64.34N 34.45E A.A. map does not extend north of Leningrad
Izmailovo, on road from Moscow to Vladimir	55.45N 47.16E Map 14 FG 34
Kiev	50.28N 30.29E Map 15 DE 45
Kize	59.01N 57.42E north-east of Glazov, not on map
Kronstadt	60.00N 29.40E Map 13 DE 56
Leningrad	59.55N 30.25E Map 13 DE 56
Moscow	55.45N 37.42E Map 13 DE 56
Petrozavodsk	61.46N 34.19E outside A.A. map area
Tsarskoye Selo (Pushkin Station)	59.42N 30.22E Map 13 DE 56
Rybinsk	58.01N 38.52E Map 14 BC 45
Sestroretsk, north-west of Leningrad	60.09N 29.58E Map 13 DE 56
Tallin	59.22N 24.48E Map 13 BC 56
Tula	54.11N 37.38E Map 13 FG 23

* *A.A. Eastern European Handbook, 1970–1*

WEST GERMANY

In 1939 it would have been fair to say that no country in Europe, including Britain, had a richer stock of technological monuments than Germany and that no country took better care of them. Both statements are still broadly true, despite the widespread destruction of the war years and the urgent demands on national resources during the post-war period. The great range of the country's industries and the long tradition of educated industrialists, first-class museums and expert attention to historical material have combined to bring about a general atmosphere of knowledgeable care which is very different from what one tends to find elsewhere. Germany also became aware a good deal earlier than most other countries that many technological activities are attractive to tourists, or can be made so. The visitor to West Germany is consequently likely to find that both the national and the local tourist organisations are well briefed about the industrial monuments which are easily accessible and particularly well worth seeing.

MUSEUMS

The Deutsches Museum in *Munich* (Museumsinsel 1) is wholly devoted to the history of industry and technology and is one of the largest and finest museums of its kind in the world. Its library publications and exhibits form the national centre for the preservation, recording and study of industrial monuments. It was severely damaged during bombing raids between 1942 and 1945, but the work of repair and renovation has been very successfully completed. Many of the objects on show are very large; they include the full-size reconstruction of a blast-furnace of 1800 from

163

the Siegerland; sections of mines; a scythe-smithy from the Black Forest (1803); a complete printing workshop of 1841 and, in the Museum gardens, a very fine thatched windmill from Ostfriesland, which was built in 1866.

Similar grand-scale exhibits are to be found in the Altona Museum in *Hamburg* (Museumstrasse 23). They include a ship-building workshop, with all its tools, a potter's workshop, a grist-mill, with its quern and horse-gear, and a complete farmhouse.

At *Kassel-Wilhelmshöhe* is the Deutsches Tapeten Museum (German Wallpaper Museum), and at *Bünde*, in Westphalia, which has had in its time no fewer than 40 tobacco factories, is the National Tobacco Museum. At *Ulm* (Fursteneckerstrasse 7) there is a museum devoted to flour and breadmaking, and the Heimatmuseum in Freibourg includes the Black Forest Museum of Clock-making, *Speyer*, in the Rhineland, has the most important museum devoted to the production of wine (Grosse Pfaffengasse 7), and other specialist industrial museums are at *Burg Altena*, in Westphalia (the German Wire Museum), *Solingen* (Cutlery Museum, Wuppertaler Strasse 160); *Offenbach* (German Shoe and Leather Museum, Frankfurter Strasse 86); *Mainz* (the former Gutenberg Museum, Liebfrauenplatz 5, for the history of printing).

The German Transport Museum (Deutsches Verkehrsmuseum, Lessingstrasse 6) is at *Nürnberg*; the German Bicycle Museum (Deutsches Zweirad Museum) is at *Neckarsulm*, near Heilbronn, and the Typewriter Museum (Schreibmaschinen Museum) at *Bayreuth*.

Most of the leading industrial concerns have an historical collection which can be visited by members of the public. One of the largest of these is the museum at Daimler-Benz, in *Stuttgart-Untertürkheim*. Just outside Stuttgart, at *Bad Cannstatt* (13, Taubenheimstrasse) is the Gottlieb Daimler Memorial. Daimler lived here and, in the small garden house beside his villa, he set up his own workshop, and in collaboration with Wilhelm Maybach, successfully developed a high-speed gasoline engine. The Volkswagen concern has a museum at *Wolfsburg*, which shows how the company developed from not very promising beginnings to its present world-wide importance.

Another important company museum is that of Siemens, the big electrical concern. It is at the Werner von Siemens Institut, 10 Prannerstrasse, *Munich 2*, and contains the Werner von Siemens Room with a number of examples of his early instruments and inventions, such as the needle telegraph.

TRANSPORT Canals

Germany has a long history of canal building. The earliest canal is the Fossa Carolina, built by Charlemagne in 793, between Rezat and the

Altmühl to form part of a Rhine-Main-Danube link. Another, but much later, royal canal was the Ludwig-Danube-Main Canal, constructed to the orders of Ludwig I of Bavaria to provide water communication between Bamberg and Kelheim. 176 kilometres long, with 100 locks, it took 10 years to build and was opened to traffic in 1845. A convenient and very pleasant point at which to visit it is *Erlangen*. The Rhine has been much canalised during the nineteenth and twentieth centuries, both by the Germans and the French. The dyked course, Basel-Mainz, is now 80.5 kilometres shorter than the natural channel. The Grand Canal d'Alsace, parallel to the Rhine, was completed by the French in 1933. The Rhine itself, on the last stretch to Basel, has since been neglected. The *Kiel Canal*, linking the Baltic and the North Sea, is somewhat misnamed in English – the Germans refer to it more accurately as the Nord Ostsee Kanal – as it runs considerably to the north of Kiel. A by-product of growing Prussian imperialism and sea-power, it was built during the 1890s to provide a rapid and secure link between the naval base at Kiel and the North Sea, but although inspired by war organisers, it now carries more vessels each day than any other ship canal in the world. It is 98.2 kilometres in length, but presented no particular engineering problems, and belongs rather more to naval than to technological history. Although the Baltic and the North Sea are at the same level, the tidal range at the North Sea end is so great that sea locks are required.

TRANSPORT Bridges and Tunnels

There is a great wealth of old bridges in Germany. Many of them are faithful reproductions, at least in part, to make good war-time destruction and damage. As good examples of medieval bridge-building we can instance the stone bridge over the Oster at *Furth* in the Saarland, built in 1200, which has four arches and a roadway 3.3 metres wide. Later (fifteenth century) and of a different type is the Nahebrucke at *Kreuznach*, which has four-storeyed houses spanning the bridge and jutting out on either side. At *Schwabisch-Hall* in Wurttemberg is the covered wooden pedestrian bridge (restored in 1790 and again after the Second World War) and the Klettensteg, a wrought-iron suspension bridge of 1836, with a span of 34 metres and a road-width of two metres.

Another eighteenth century roofed bridge is to be seen at *Unterregenbach* in South Germany. It was restored in 1950. *Rothenburg-an-der-Tauber* has a curious two-tiered bridge; the lower part was built in 1330 and the upper in 1400. Both levels are of stone.

Many of the more remarkable nineteenth-century bridges were natural targets for bombing raids and equally natural victims of German explosive charges, placed to delay the approaching Allied armies. Two of the best known of these damaged, but subsequently restored, bridges are the rail bridge over the Rhine at *Kehl*, and the Rhine bridge at *Koblenz*. The Kehl bridge, a girder bridge, carries two railtracks and was built by Benkiser and Keller for the Bädische Staatsbahn in 1858–60. Each end was designed to resemble the portico of a Gothic cathedral, complete with spires. The Rhine bridge at Koblenz, a graceful three-span iron bridge, is slightly later, 1862–64. It was built by Hartwich and Harkort as a rail bridge but was afterwards converted to take only road traffic.

The elegant Kaiser-Wilhelm Brücke, spanning the Inner Harbour at *Wilhelmshaven* is one of the largest swing-bridges in Europe; opened to traffic in 1909, it carries a roadway and two footpaths.

The tunnel under the River Elbe at *Hamburg* has remarkable architectural, as well as technical features. It was built between 1907 and 1911 and leaves the city side of the river not far from the St Pauli landing-stages. The entrances at both ends of the tunnel are monumental. There are two separate tunnels, each one-way, and covering the concrete lining there are majolica tiles, with a ceramic frieze and reliefs. The St Pauli landing-stages were built at the same time as the tunnel, 1907–9, and are also scheduled as a technical monument. The centre section was destroyed by bombing, but has been restored in the original style.

TRANSPORT   Docks

In the old docks at *Hamburg*, at a place known as Beim Neuen Krahn, is a famous crane of the medieval type which had the jib projecting from a kind of round pavilion (see plate 12). The Hamburg crane, 'the New Crane', was installed in 1858, to replace an older wooden crane, of a very similar design, which fell to pieces the previous year. Earlier examples of the same of crane are to be seen, in a good state of preservation, at *Würzburg* and *Trier*. The Trier crane was built in 1413. It can raise a load of 2,500 kilogrammes, which is probably much less than its original capacity. The Wurzburg crane, built in 1722, has two jibs, of which the larger has a lifting capacity of 2,000 kilogrammes.

TRANSPORT   Railways

The German railway system was very heavily damaged during the 1939–1945 war, and none of the major railway stations escaped undamaged. The oldest surviving railway station in Germany is in *Brunswick*, built in 1843–44 by Karl Theodor Ottmer. It is no longer in use as a station and in 1960 it was bought by the Braunschweigische Staatsbank, who restored it after war-time damage and achieved a very successful conversion to its new purpose. The overhead railway at *Wuppertal*, with the coaches suspended from the rails, is a much treasured item of German railway engineering. It was built in 1901 and survived the Second World War more or less intact; the coaches are new and the stations have been a good deal rebuilt and modernised.

WINDMILLS

The North of Germany once depended on windmills almost as much as Holland and there are many interesting survivals, especially in the flat countryside in Ostfriesland and Schleswig-Holstein. One of the oldest mills is at *Dornum*, a post-mill dating from 1628. Most of the mills of this age were burnt during the wars of 1622–24. Dornum Mill is now owned by the local historical society, the Ostfriesische Landschaft. The Wind and Watermill Society in Ostfriesland is a very active body, which has been responsible for preserving and restoring a number of fine mills in this part of Germany. One of the strangest mills in Germany is at *Hüven*, which was erected in the seventeenth century as a watermill, and had a windmill added to it in 1802. The whole structure fell into serious decay, but it has now been fully restored.

SILVER MINING

Germany has much to offer anyone interested in the history of mining. There are mining museums at *Bochum* in Westphalia, and at *Bexbach*, in Saarland. Perhaps the mine best known to tourists is the Samson silver-mine at *St Andreasberg* in the Harz, which was worked between 1521 and 1910. The surface installations, which can be visited, include the wooden shaft building, the Gaifel; the adjoining rope drift, or haulage road; and the stamp-battery room, driven by an overshot waterwheel which is fitted with two opposed bucket rings, allowing the wheel to be rotated in either direction. The Samson buildings were restored in 1958.

The drainage of the mines in the Harz and the Ruhr presented serious problems, not only in removing water from the mines, but in getting it away afterwards. Long channels were constructed for the purpose, often involving much tunnelling. A good example of one of these gravity drainage schemes can be seen at *Essen-Hardenstein*, in the Ruhrtal. This is the St Johannes drainage canal, which is 3,170 metres long and was completed in 1804. It went out of use with the introduction of first steam-driven and then electric pumps, and with the movement of mining activities away towards the northern plain.

COAL MINING

Coal has been extracted in the Ruhr area since the fourteenth century, but production was intensified during the last quarter of the eighteenth century to meet the demands of the new saltworks at Unna. Once coal began to be extensively used in the smelting of iron, the scale of coal-mining operations was transformed. Relics of a number of the mid-nineteenth century mining enterprises are still to be seen in the Ruhr, among them the pit-head buildings at *Essen-Altendorf, Bochum* and *Essen-Borbeck*. The Altendorf pit reached a depth of 530 metres; the Preussich Szepter pit, to the south of Bochum, dates from 1874 and reaches 150 metres; while the Christian Levin pit, at Essen-Borbeck, goes back to 1843. Internally, the pit-head buildings have been much modified, but from outside they still have much the same appearance as a century ago.

SALT MINING

Salt has been extensively mined in Bavaria and Württemberg since the seventeenth century. There is a famous salt-mine at *Berchtesgaden*, which can be visited, and others nearby at *Rosenheim, Bad Reichenhall* and *Trauntsein*. This group of Bavarian saltmines is linked together with a pipe-line that carries the brine from one centre to another, as production and the drying process demand. Reichenhall has two large waterwheels to pump brine, each 13 metres in diameter, which were installed in 1835. Those taking part in the guided tours of the Alte Saline (old Salt-Works) at Bad Reichenhall are lent protective clothing.

IRON WORKS

The history of the Ruhr can be studied in the Ruhrland Museum in *Essen*. Industrially, it is not a long history; in 1758 the Antoni foundry in Oberhausen-Sterkrade built the first pig-iron plant in the area, using charcoal as a fuel. In 1799 the first steam-engine, known as Wasserkunst, was set up at the Vollmund pit near Bochum. The first blast furnace, fired with coke made from Ruhr coal, went into operation at Mülheim in 1849.

Much of the history of the Ruhr is embodied in the old ironworks, the Luisenhütte at *Essen-Wocklum* (see plate 39). This is a very old iron-working area. The ironworks at Wocklum were dormant during the Thirty Years War (1618–48) and were brought back into operation early in the following century by the owner, Freiherr Franz Ferdinand von Landsberg. The premises were rebuilt and the furnace enlarged in 1833–34 and again in 1854, when power was provided by a steam engine, instead of a water-wheel. In 1935 the Hütte was in poor condition and the owner, unable to maintain it, gave it to the local authority, on a 99 year lease, with the condition that they should restore it and open it to the public. To make this possible, an appeal was launched by the Association of German Engineers and the work was eventually completed in 1958.

A number of eighteenth-century forges have survived in Germany, with their water-driven hammers. A forge in a good state of repair is at *Essen-Margarethental*. Also in Essen is the historical collection relating to the Krupp concern. It is housed in part of the Villa Hügel, the former residence of the Krupp family. Most of this interesting collection consists of documents, photographs and models.

GAS AND WATERWORKS

Most of the early buildings and plant connected with public utilities – water, gas and electricity – in Germany were severely damaged or destroyed during the war. *Hamburg* Gasworks, on the Grasbrook, for instance, pioneered the use of gas for lighting streets in Germany. The works was built in 1844 by English engineers and Hamburg streets were first lit with gas in October 1845. London (1814), Paris (1815) and Vienna (1817) had gas lighting much earlier. The buildings and gasholder at Grasbrook were a noted harbour landmark. Only the gasholder was rebuilt (1951). The ruins of the other structures were swept away and replaced by modern equipment, employing natural gas and oil, not coal.

The Rothenburgsort Waterworks in *Hamburg* were more fortunate. They are no longer in use, but are preserved as a technological monument. Built in 1849, to a design by the English engineer W. Lindley, they were enlarged in 1833–35 and 1903–9. The tower is particularly distinguished.

LIGHTHOUSE

Practically the only technological monuments to escape the war with little damage were lighthouses, which are difficult and rather pointless to hit from the air. The medieval lighthouse on the island of *Neuwerk*, near Cuxhaven, is still in use. Its square tower was built *c.* 1300, but the lantern on top is more modern, built in two stages in 1814 and 1875.

Location of sites - **West Germany***

Bad Reichenhall	47.43N	12.53E	Map 15 BC 23
Berchtesgaden	47.38N	13.00E	Map 15 BC 23
Bexbach, east of Völklingen	49.15N	6.51E	Map 14 BC 45
Bochum	51.28N	7.11E	Map 11 BC 34
Brunswick	52.15N	10.30E	Map 11 EF 45
Dornum, north-west of Aurich	53.39N	7.26E	Map 9 BC 23
Erlangen	49.36N	11.02E	Map 14 FG 56
Essen	51.27N	6.57E	Map 11 BC 34
Essen-Altendorf	51.27N	6.57E	Map 11 BC 34
Essen-Borbeck	51.27N	6.57E	Map 11 BC 34
Essen-Hardenstein	51.27N	6.57E	Map 11 BC 34
Essen-Margarethental	51.27N	6.57E	Map 11 BC 34
Essen-Wocklum	51.27N	6.57E	Map 11 BC 34
Furth, north-east of Saarlouis	49.20N	6.46E	Map 13 BC 45
Hamburg	53.33N	10.00E	Map 9 DE 23
Hüven, north-north-west of Aurich	53.41N	7.27E	Map 9 BC 23
Kehl	49.35N	7.50E	Map 14 CD 34
Kiel Canal, (Leversau, north of Kiel)	54.22N	10.05E	Map 9 DE 34
Koblenz	50.21N	7.36E	Map 11 CD 12
Kreuznach	49.52N	7.51E	Map 14 CD 56
Neuwerk, island north-west of Cuxhaven	53.56N	8.32E	Map 9 CD 23 (not marked)
Rosenheim	47.51N	12.09E	Map 15 AB 23
Rothenburg-an-der-Tauber	49.23N	10.03E	Map 14 EF 45
Schwäbisch Hall	49.07N	9.45E	Map 14 EF 45
St Andreasberg, south-west of Braunlage	51.30N	10.42E	Map 11 FG 34
Traunstein	47.52N	12.39E	Map 15 BC 23
Triberg	48.07N	8.14E	Map 14 CD 23
Trier	49.45N	6.39E	Map 14 BC 56

Ulm	38.24N	10.00E	Map 14 EF 34
Unterregenbach, west of Dingolfing	48.28N	12.33E	Map 15 BC 45
Wilhelmshaven	53.32N	8.07E	Map 9 CD 23
Wuppertal	51.15N	7.10E	Map 11 BC 23
Würzburg	49.48N	9.57E	Map 14 EF 56

* A.A. Continental Handbook, 1970–1

YUGOSLAVIA

Yugoslavia now has a population of a little over 20 million. On the eve of the Second World War, the total was 16 million, but the huge losses in human lives during the war, about 1.7 million, and a reduced birthrate produced an absolute decrease in the population.

Over the same period there have been great structural changes in employment. In 1939 75 per cent. of the working population was engaged in agriculture, while today the figure is below 50 per cent. The pre-war economy was backward, and although Yugoslavia is very rich in metallic ores and in coal, in 1939 manufacturing industry and mining provided less than 20 per cent. of the national income, which stagnated during the inter-war years. Between 1941 and 1945 this already poor country lost 223 of its mines, 40 per cent. of its industrial plants and 52 per cent. of its railways. This destruction was made good during the first five-year plan (1947–52) and since then progress has been very rapid.

Broadly speaking, however, the post-war change from a mainly agricultural to a mainly industrial country, combined with the bombing, burning and looting of so much of the existing plant, has meant that Yugoslavia has few industrial monuments earlier than the late 1940s and early 1950s. These were the years of the country's first real industrial revolution and the factories built within that period are Yugoslavia's true industrial monuments. The majority of industries are in the north-western part of the country.

MUSEUMS

Yugoslavia has an excellent system of regional museums, the best being at *Banja Luka, Brežice, Celje, Cetinje, Llubljana, Maribor, Ptuj, Split* and *Zagreb*. Each of these museums devotes considerable attention to the historical development of the region in question and, following the normal modern practice in Eastern Europe, there is a strong emphasis on political and economic history.

Examples of the old, small-scale rural technology can be found at the museum at *Škofja Loka* Castle, and especially in the museum's open-air section. The National Technical Museum at *Zagreb* (Slavska C. 18) was established in 1954, and there is another new museum, the Railway Museum, at *Belgrade* (Nemanjina ulica 6) (1950). Two of the oldest museums are the maritime museums at *Dubrovnik* (St John's Fortress) (1872) and at *Kotor*.

MINING

The deposits of both non-ferrous and iron ores are among the richest and most extensive in Europe. Yugoslavia produces more copper and bismuth than any other European country, and holds second place for silver and third for bauxite. The copper mining and smelting works at *Bor* in Serbia have been important since the 1920s, although the history of mining in the area goes back to prehistoric times. Photographs taken in 1905 show only a small settlement of wooden buildings, but there was considerable development during the next ten years, mostly with French capital. The installations were almost totally destroyed during the war and, historically, the most interesting piece of archaeology to be seen there is the plaque commemorating the handing-over of the plant to the control of the workers in 1964. Similar plaques are to be found at many other factories in Yugoslavia, marking a turning point in the industrial history of the country.

Yugoslavia has had a flourishing mining and metal industry since the thirteenth century, although the scale of it remained very small until comparatively recently. A good example of the change of scale can be noticed at *Jesenice*, where the large post-war ironworks is on virtually the same site as the medieval workings, and at the *Trepča* lead works, which has a long tradition and is now one of the most important in Europe. The most important iron-mines are at *Valeš* and *Ljubija* in Bosnia.

SHIPBUILDING

The same kind of development has taken place in shipbuilding. In 1939 all the shipyards were small, and concerned mainly with overhauls, while today there are twenty maritime and river shipyards, with a large building programme. The largest of these enterprises are the Uljanik shipyards at *Pula*, the Treći Maj shipyards at *Rijeka* and the *Split* shipyards, all of which have grown from very small pre-war establishments. The river shipyards are along the Danube and Sava, and are mostly developments of pre-war sites.

ZINC AND RUBBER

One of the oldest industrial plants in Yugoslavia is the Cinkasna zinc works at *Celje*, established in 1873. It survived the war more or less intact, and has been greatly enlarged and modernised since 1945. A large modern factory with a long pedigree and humble beginnings is the Sava rubber factory at *Kranj*, which before the war was little more than a handicraft workshop.

TEXTILES

The carpet industry centred at *Mostar* in the Pirst specialises on hand-woven carpets for export. The weaving sheds have not been greatly modernised and preserve much of their old atmosphere and techniques. This is not the case with the cotton-textile industry, which is situated mainly in the *Zagreb* and *Belgrade* areas. Some of the least damaged of the pre-war mills here have been restored, but the industry is mostly carried on now in new buildings. A considerable proportion of the raw cotton used is home-grown, in Macedonia.

TOBACCO

Tobacco is extensively grown in Yugoslavia, with one of the principal centres in *Zletovo*. A characteristic feature of the tobacco-growing areas are the little square brick and tile sheds in which the leaf is stored for drying.

WINE

Yugoslavia is an important wine-producing country. Production has been industrialised since the war with large new plants and cellars at *Ormož*, *Umag*, *Rijeka*, *Vršac* and *Gruda*, near Dubrovnik. Some of these new buildings, at Vršac and Gruda especially, are excellent examples of modern industrial architecture. The old type of cellarage, above ground and looking rather like fire-stations without doors, can be seen at *Topola*, and *Potmoje*. At *Maribor* there are fine vaulted cellars, containing monumental storage casks, similar to those to be found in the Trentino district of Italy. Other majestic cellars are still in use at *Kučevo*.

TIMBER

About a third of the total area of Yugoslvaia is covered by forest. Before the war, production was almost entirely of sawn timber and poles. This part of the industry is still important, but since 1952 a dozen paper and pulp mills have been built, creating what was for Yugoslavia an entirely new industry. These mills are located mainly in Bosnia and Herzegovina.

RAILWAYS

At a time when railway lines are being closed all over Western Europe it is interesting to note that Yugoslavia has had a large programme of railway building since 1945, as an essential part of the post-war industrialisation of the country. There are 1,250 more miles of railway now than in 1939.

Location of sites - Yugoslavia*

Belgrade	44.50N 20.30E	Map 7	AB 34
Bor	44.05N 22.06E	Map 7	BC 12
Celje	46.15N 15.16E	Map 6	BC 45
Gruda	42.31N 18.22E	Map 8	CD 45
Jesenice, north-east of Bled	46.26N 14.02E	Map 6	AB 45

176

Kranj	46.15N	14.20E	Map 6	AB 45
Kučevo	44.30N	21.40E	Map 7	AB 23
Ljubija	44.55N	16.35E	Map 6	CD 23
Maribor	46.35N	15.40E	Map 6	BC 45
Mostar	43.20N	17.50E	Map 6	DE 12
Ormož	46.25N	16.10E	Map 6	CD 45
Potomje, south of Zaba	42.56N	17.20E	Map 8	BC 45
Pula	44.52N	13.52E	Map 6	AB 45
Rijeka	45.20N	14.27E	Map 6	AB 34
Split	43.31N	16.28E	Map 6	CD 12
Topola	44.15N	20.41E	Map 7	AB 12
Trepča	42.56N	20.55E	Map 8	EF 45
Umag	45.26N	13.31E	Map 6	AB 34
Valeš	44.10N	18.20E	Map 6	DE 23
Vršac	45.07N	21.19E	Map 7	AB 23
Zagreb	45.48N	15.58E	Map 6	CD 45
Zletovo	41.59N	22.15E	Map 8	FG 34

* *A.A. Eastern European Handbook, 1970–1*

Index